Body-Mind Blueprint

Strategies for Synchronized Health

by
Well-Being Publishing

WELL-BEING
PUBLISHING

Body-Mind Blueprint

Strategies for Synchronized Health

Contents

Introduction 1

Chapter 1: The Foundation of the Body-Mind Blueprint 4
  Understanding Holistic Health 4
  Physiology Meets Psychology: An Integrated Approach 7

Chapter 2: The Science Behind the Synchrony 11
  Exploring Psychophysiological Research 11
  How Emotions Shape Our Physiology 14

Chapter 3: Nourishing the Body, Nourishing the Mind 18
  The Role of Nutrition in Mental Wellness 18
  Creating a Balanced Diet for Physical and Mental Health 21

Chapter 4: Movement as Medicine 25
  The Psychological Effects of Exercise 25
  Incorporating Mindful Movement into Daily Life 29

Chapter 5: Mastering Stress Management 32
  Stress-Reduction Techniques That Really Work 32
  Building Resilience: Turning Stress Into Strength 36

Chapter 6: The Art and Science of Sleep 39
  Understanding Sleep's Role in Mental Health 39
  Creating a Sleep-Conducive Environment 43

Chapter 7: Mindfulness and Meditation 46
  Cultivating Awareness for Mental and Physical Health 47
  Practical Applications of Mindfulness in Daily Life 50

Chapter 8: Emotional Balance for Physical Wellbeing........................ 54
The Impact of Mental Health on Disease and Immunity 54
Psychosomatic Medicine: Healing from Within............................ 58

Chapter 9: Lifelong Learning for Lifelong Health 62
The Impact of Mental Stimulation on Brain Health 62
Adopting a Growth Mindset.. 66

Chapter 10: Community and Connection 69
Social Support as a Pillar of Health 69
The Health Benefits of Altruism and Volunteering 73

Chapter 11: Integrative and Complementary Therapies 76
Overview of Alternative Health Practices...................................... 76
Finding the Right Balance in Integrative Care 80

Chapter 12: Crafting Your Personal Body-Mind Blueprint 83
Setting Goals for Synchronized Health.. 83
Monitoring Progress and Adjusting Strategically............................ 86

Harmonizing the Body- Mind Symphony 88

Appendix A: Appendix.. 91
A: Resources for Further Learning 91
B: Body-Mind Blueprint Worksheets 94

C: Glossary of Terms... 98

References.. 101

Introduction

The interplay between the body and mind is a rich and intricate tapestry, woven through centuries of human experience and scientific discovery. In our modern era, understanding this connection is more important than ever, as we endeavor to bridge the gap between physical health and mental well-being. This book, "Unlocking the Body-Mind Connection," delves into the profound relationship between our psychological state and physical health, offering insights and practical tools to enhance overall well-being.

For a long time, Western medicine has tended to separate the body from the mind, treating them as distinct entities. However, emerging research increasingly supports a holistic view, recognizing the symbiosis between our mental states and physical health. Studies have shown that stress, anxiety, and emotional upheavals can manifest as physical symptoms, while physical ailments can exacerbate or trigger psychological distress (Pascoe et al., 2017). This duality underscores the necessity of understanding the body-mind connection.

Imagine your body as an orchestra. Each system plays its part, contributing to a harmonious symphony that is your overall health. If one section falls out of tune, the entire composition is affected. Similarly, an imbalance in the mind can reverberate through the body, manifesting as fatigue, pain, or illness. Conversely, a healthy, aligned mental state can inspire physical vigor and resilience.

Incorporating an integrative approach into health care practice is no longer just an option; it's essential. Professionals increasingly recognize that mental and physical health interventions need to be intertwined. This realization has led to broader acceptance of holistic practices that encompass not just symptom treatment, but the nurturing of mind, body, and spirit (Björnsdóttir, 2020). Health care providers, from therapists to physiotherapists, are now adopting strategies that leverage this connection to foster healing and well-being.

The connection between body and mind is also echoed in cultural traditions across the globe. Ancient philosophies like Ayurveda and Traditional Chinese Medicine have long acknowledged this link, prescribing treatments that balance the body's energies and promote psychological equilibrium. These traditional systems emphasize prevention, understanding that maintaining this balance can avert disease and promote long-lasting health (Lin et al., 2019).

One of the most fascinating aspects of the body-mind connection is its adaptability. While genetic predispositions and environmental factors play their roles, our thoughts, feelings, and behaviors exert significant influence over our health. This fact is both empowering and enlightening. It means that by cultivating positive mental states and engaging in mindful practices, we can actively steer our physical health in a favorable direction. Personal growth, then, becomes not just a mental pursuit but a comprehensive strategy for holistic well-being.

Throughout the following chapters, we'll explore various facets of this multifaceted relationship. From understanding the physiological mechanisms linking our emotions to our bodies, to practical steps for nurturing this connection through nutrition, movement, and mindfulness, this book offers a roadmap for those seeking to optimize their health through a more integrated approach.

We'll delve into the scientific research that underpins this connection, shedding light on the biopsychosocial models that illustrate how intertwined our mental and physical lives are. This understanding is crucial in fostering a comprehensive view of health that honors both the body and the mind as equally influential to our overall state of being.

Furthermore, we'll explore the role of community and connection, and how they serve as vital pillars supporting both mental and physical health. The human need for social bonds and interconnectedness is fundamental, and the health benefits of such relationships extend far beyond emotional support. They play a critical role in reducing stress, enhancing recovery, and improving longevity.

Ultimately, this book aims to empower you. By unlocking the mysteries of the body-mind connection, you'll be equipped with the knowledge to make informed decisions about your health. You'll be inspired to embrace a lifestyle that reflects both awareness and intention, one that fosters a harmonious relationship between your body and mind. Each chapter is crafted to guide you toward a deeper understanding and to offer tangible strategies that you can incorporate into your daily life.

The journey towards holistic health is dynamic and deeply personal. It's about setting intentions, making conscious choices, and embracing the interconnectedness of your being. As you turn the pages, open yourself to the possibilities that lie within the body-mind connection and envision a life where health and happiness coexist seamlessly.

Join us on this path of discovery and growth as we embark on a transformative journey, uncovering not just the science and theory behind the body-mind connection, but its practical applications and profound impact on our everyday lives. Welcome to a world where health is a dynamic balance of mental and physical, where vitality is the norm, and where a thriving life awaits you.

Chapter 1: The Foundation of the Body-Mind Blueprint

At the heart of understanding holistic health is recognizing the intricate symphony between our physical bodies and mental realms, an intersection where physiology meets psychology. This junction isn't just a place where anatomy and emotion occasionally brush shoulders; it's the very cradle of our wellbeing, where each influences and refines the other. In nurturing this body-mind connection, we lay the groundwork for a health approach that respects the complexity of human experience. Research underscores the seamless integration of these systems, revealing that emotions can direct physiological responses just as physical conditions impact our mental states (Kabat-Zinn, 2013; Sapolsky, 2004). This interconnected perspective empowers us, offering a tapestry of healing that is as diverse and dynamic as life itself. It's more than a path to health; it's a journey of self-discovery and a testament to the body's innate wisdom, urging us to listen and respond to its cues for genuine transformation and growth.

Understanding Holistic Health

Holistic health is more than just a catchphrase; it's a profound understanding of the way different aspects of our lives intertwine. It embodies the idea that for us to achieve optimal wellbeing, we need to consider not just our physical health, but our mental, emotional, and spiritual well-being too. This comprehensive approach integrates the entire being, recognizing that each component influences and is influenced by the others.

At its core, holistic health acknowledges that the whole is greater than the sum of its parts. This perspective encourages individuals to see beyond symptoms and ailments of the body or mind as isolated instances. Instead, it prompts a deeper inquiry: What's really going on beneath the surface? This inquiry is essential because the roots of what ails us are often deeper than they appear, encompassing diet, lifestyle, thoughts, environment, and even relationships. Addressing these elements comprehensively untangles the complexities of health and opens the door to genuine healing and transformation (Smith & White, 2020).

Holistic health integrates various therapeutic disciplines and wellness practices to promote total health. These can include conventional medicine practices, but also complementary therapies such as acupuncture, yoga, meditation, and nutrition. Each practice plays a role in nurturing the mind-body connection, helping individuals repair what modern life often erodes. Practices like mindfulness and meditation, for instance, are not just beneficial for mental clarity, but also for lowering stress levels and boosting immunity (Davidson et al., 2003). Similarly, maintaining a balanced diet rich in plant-based foods and essential nutrients directly impacts both physical health and mental acuity (Jacka et al., 2014).

A key tenet of holistic health is the focus on prevention, a concept often at odds with traditional healthcare systems that tend to prioritize treating diseases over preventing them. Prevention requires a proactive approach, encouraging regular self-care practices such as exercise, healthy eating, and stress management. It's about tuning in to our bodies and minds to recognize early signs of imbalance before they escalate into more severe conditions. This proactive mindset shifts the narrative from merely surviving to truly thriving.

One of the most inspiring aspects of holistic health is its emphasis on personal empowerment. By recognizing that our choices heavily influence our wellbeing, we take an active role in our health journey. This empowerment is vital; it encourages you to seek knowledge, ask questions, and make informed decisions about your wellness journey. It's about reclaiming ownership of your health by understanding your body's signals and responding holistically.

Furthermore, holistic health emphasizes connection. Human beings are intrinsically social creatures, and our connections with others significantly influence our health. Studies have shown that strong social ties can lead to longer life, improved mental health, and quicker recovery from illness (Holt-Lunstad et al., 2010). Thus, fostering relationships and being part of a community is integral to holistic wellbeing, providing support, joy, and purpose.

Understanding holistic health also involves addressing mental health with the same seriousness and commitment as physical health. Mental health should never be an afterthought; it is foundational to how we experience and engage with the world. Holistic health practices often include therapy, counseling, or other mental health services to deal with emotional trauma, stress, or mental illness. The goal is to cultivate a balanced emotional state that supports overall health and wellbeing.

It's important to note that spiritual health, though often overlooked, holds a crucial position in the holistic model. Spiritual health doesn't necessarily refer to religious practices but rather a sense of purpose and meaning in life. This element of holistic health can be nurtured through practices like meditation, reflection, and connection to nature, promoting a sense of inner peace and fulfillment.

Adopting a holistic approach isn't about abandoning modern medicine; it's about expanding it to accommodate a fuller picture of health. It calls for an integrative approach where conventional treatments are complemented by alternative methods, forming a personalized health strategy tailored to one's unique needs and circumstances. In this way, holistic health not only aids in healing physical ailments but also encourages an enriched quality of life.

In essence, holistic health teaches us that our body and mind are not separate entities but rather an interconnected ecosystem. Our thoughts, emotions, and physical states are in constant communication, and by paying attention to this dialogue, we gain valuable insights into our overall health. This understanding empowers us to lead lives that are not only healthy but also deeply rewarding.

As we continue exploring the body-mind blueprint, remember that each step forward is a stride toward a more harmonious and holistic existence. It's a journey of self-discovery and empowerment, paving the path to a healthier and more integrated self. The notion of holistic health invites us to rise to our full potential, not just as individuals but as part of a larger community striving for wellness in every sense of the word.

Physiology Meets Psychology: An Integrated Approach

When we explore the intricate dance of physiology and psychology, we're met with a profound realization: the body and mind are not merely interwoven but symbiotic. Through the lens of integrative health, we see that physical and mental well-being form a cohesive unit, each relying on the other for optimal health and functionality. The idea that our physical processes underpin psychological experiences is not just a whim of modern wellness rhetoric but a scientifically backed perspective.

Consider the role of neurotransmitters, the chemical messengers of the brain. Dopamine, serotonin, and other neurotransmitters not only influence our mood and emotions but are also closely linked to various physiological processes. Serotonin, for instance, is often dubbed the "happiness hormone," yet approximately 90% of it is found in the gut, highlighting a fascinating connection between emotional well-being and digestive function (Gershon, 1999). This exemplifies how intricately physiology and psychology are linked, but also how adopting an integrative approach can promote healing and enhance vitality.

In the realm of medicine, the bridge linking mental and physical states is increasingly being recognized. Psychoneuroimmunology, a field that examines the interaction between psychological processes and the nervous and immune systems, provides compelling evidence of this interplay. Stress, a psychological phenomenon, can weaken immune responses, making the body more susceptible to disease (Ader, Felten, & Cohen, 1991). Understanding these connections makes clear that nurturing the mind is central to supporting the body's defense mechanisms, just as caring for the body aids in stabilizing mental health.

The rhythms of daily life, governed by both external schedules and internal biological clocks, further illustrate this interconnectedness. The circadian rhythm, our internal timekeeper, significantly impacts both physiological functions and psychological states. When aligned properly, it supports physical health by optimizing hormone production, digestion, and sleep cycles. However, disruptions to this natural rhythm, such as from irregular sleep patterns or chronic stress, can lead to a cascade of health issues, including mood disorders and metabolic problems (Arendt, 2010).

Breath is another potent link between body and mind. Pranayama, a practice found in yoga that focuses on breath control, exemplifies the impact physiological practice has on psychological well-being. Slow, deliberate breathing can activate the parasympathetic nervous system, inducing relaxation and diminishing stress hormones like cortisol (Brown & Gerbarg, 2009). Thus, through deliberate physiological practice, we can positively affect our psychological state.

Moreover, the psychological notion of self-efficacy, a belief in one's ability to succeed, has tangible physiological outcomes. High levels of self-efficacy enhance immune function, improve cardiovascular health, and promote longevity (Bandura, 1997). This relationship showcases how psychological empowerment can drive physiological resilience, reinforcing the importance of fostering mental fortitude as a pillar of health.

The expression of emotions and their physiological repercussions paints another compelling picture of the body-mind partnership. Anger can elevate blood pressure, grief can manifest as chest pain, and chronic happiness detracts stress impacts and promotes a state conducive to wellness (Sapolsky, 2004). Therefore, managing emotions serves as both a balm for psychological unease and a preventative measure for physical ailments.

Take stress, an unavoidable part of life, yet how we process it is critical. Chronic stress entails prolonged exposure to cortisol, known to impair memory, weaken bones, and suppress the immune system (McEwen & Stellar, 1993). By engaging in practices that promote psychological resilience, like mindfulness or cognitive behavioral techniques, we can mitigate these physiological stresses and encourage bodily harmony.

Thus, physiology and psychology don't just co-exist; they engage in an exquisite symbiosis that demands attention and refinement. This integrated approach empowers individuals by enhancing awareness of the body-mind connection to cultivate practices that enrich well-being on all fronts. By harmonizing the physiological and psychological, we foster an environment of holistic health, unlocking potential and maximizing wellness.

As we navigate the complexities of life, reinforcing this understanding is paramount. The quest for health and balance isn't a singular journey; it's an ongoing dialogue between our bodies and minds. Through compassion, education, and proactive engagement, we can nurture this dialogue, promoting a synergy that fortifies resilience and vitality.

The journey of integrating physiology with psychology isn't just a personal endeavor—it's a call to transform traditional paradigms of health into more inclusive, cohesive frameworks. It's about recognizing that our bodies and minds are not isolated islands but continents connected by bridges of habit and thought, each influencing the other in profound, transformative ways. As we harness this understanding, we afford ourselves the tools to live fuller, healthier lives.

Chapter 2: The Science Behind the Synchrony

In the intricate dance of life, understanding the synchrony between our bodies and minds is pivotal for unlocking a holistic approach to health. The foundation of this synchrony lies in a fascinating interplay of biological and psychological processes. Psychophysiological research has begun to unravel the complex connections, revealing how intertwined our emotions and physical states really are. Take, for instance, the brain-gut axis, which showcases a bidirectional exchange of information where our inner emotional landscapes can influence digestive health and vice versa (Mayer et al., 2015). This highlights that what we often consider as separate—the physical and mental realms—are frequently just two aspects of the same phenomenon. Delving deeper, studies have shown that emotions can directly shape our physiological responses, with stress impacting everything from hormone levels to immune function (Kiecolt-Glaser et al., 2010). By understanding these dynamics, we don't just aim to remedy ailments but seek a balanced state where the body and mind work in harmony, potentially enhancing well-being in unprecedented ways. The science behind this synchrony is not merely academic; it's a call to action to foster deeper awareness and integration in our daily lives, driving us toward a more vibrant existence.

Exploring Psychophysiological Research

In the realm of psychophysiological research, we uncover the fascinating interplay between our mental and physical states, illuminating the intricate dance of science and personal transformation. At the heart of this exploration lies a profound understanding of how our thoughts, emotions, and physiological responses are inextricably linked, forming a symphony within our bodies that either harmonizes or disrupts our health (Berntson & Cacioppo, 2007). This field provides compelling evidence that our mental wellness is not only a philosophical concept but a measurable biological process, influencing everything from the beat of our hearts to the efficiency of our digestive systems. Psychophysiological research empowers us with the knowledge that stress, joy, and even fleeting emotional states can induce tangible changes in our bodily functions, urging us to adopt mindful practices that cultivate resilience and wellness (Thayer et al., 2012). By integrating these insights into daily life, individuals can embark on a holistic journey towards balance and vitality, making conscious choices that resonate deeply across their mind and body (Critchley & Nagai, 2013).

The Brain-Gut Axis: A Two-Way Street serves as a pivotal gateway to understanding the profound interplay between neurological and digestive systems, a connection that's increasingly recognized by modern science. This cross-talk between the brain and the gut isn't just a one-way directive. It's a dynamic two-way street that influences both cognitive well-being and physical health. This section delves into the array of psychophysiological research that uncovers how these two systems communicate and co-regulate, providing an illuminating glimpse into the interconnectedness at the heart of our holistic existence.

Imagine your gut and brain in a constant dialogue, sharing information and responding to the whispers and cries of the other. This communication network, known as the brain-gut axis, consists of a bidirectional pathway that includes neural, hormonal, and immunological routes. It's fascinating to think that within this conversation, our emotions can shape digestive activity and, conversely, our gut health can influence our mood and mental state (Mayer, 2011).

Researchers have long been intrigued by this axis, driven by the observation that patients with gastrointestinal disorders often suffer from mood disorders like depression and anxiety. This correlation has led to groundbreaking studies that explore the microbiome's role—a community of trillions of bacteria that inhabit our gut. These microorganisms engage in an intricate dance with our body, affecting neurotransmitter levels, such as serotonin, which is instrumental in regulating mood (Cryan & Dinan, 2012).

In the realm of psychophysiological research, scientists employ various methodologies to dissect these mechanisms. One prominent approach involves neuroimaging techniques to visualize how the brain responds to gut-related stimuli. Such studies reveal that the gut can impact regions of the brain linked to emotion processing and stress management. Furthermore, interventions aimed at gut health, like probiotics, have shown promise in alleviating symptoms of anxiety and depression, indicating a potential therapeutic pathway (Tillisch et al., 2013).

Understanding the brain-gut axis is not limited to scientific inquiry; it opens a doorway to potential strategies that integrate care for both mind and body. For those seeking personal development or stress management, it encourages a reconsideration of diet and mental health practices as interconnected rather than isolated domains. This holistic view reinforces the notion that nurturing one's gut can be just as vital as nurturing one's mind, with each facet driving improvements in the other.

But why does this relationship matter? For wellness enthusiasts and healthcare professionals alike, appreciating the brain-gut connection offers a more comprehensive framework for improving holistic health. The axis suggests that optimizing one's mental state can aid in reducing gastrointestinal symptoms, which is especially relevant for stress-induced disorders. Similarly, improving gut flora through diet can bolster emotional resilience and cognitive functioning, propelling individuals toward a balanced state of being.

The intricacies of this two-way street continue to unfold through ongoing research, which is expanding our understanding of the psychophysiology underpinning the brain-gut axis. Each new discovery invites a transformational shift in the way we perceive health, urging us to embrace a model that honors the innate dialogue between the brain and the gut. It challenges us to be curious, to explore, and to apply these insights to enhance the synchrony of body and mind.

The dance between the brain and gut is a testament to nature's complexity and inherent wisdom. While it's tempting to focus on one aspect of health, the brain-gut axis reminds us that true wellness emerges from nurturing our entire being. By adopting this broader perspective, individuals can craft more effective approaches to personal wellness, tapping into the biological symphony at the core of our existence.

In conclusion, "The Brain-Gut Axis: A Two-Way Street" chapter offers a profound insight into the mutual influences of our neurological and gastrointestinal systems, placing the reader at the edge of an immersive journey into holistic health. By weaving scientific understanding with practical application, this section empowers individuals to redefine their approach to health, and to craft a thoughtful integration of mind and body practices for a harmonious life.

How Emotions Shape Our Physiology

The intricate relationship between our emotions and physiology is like a beautifully choreographed dance, constantly in motion and deeply interconnected. As research delves deeper into this dynamic interrelationship, it's becoming ever more apparent how emotions can drive physiological changes and, conversely, how our physical state can influence our emotions. This complex dance has profound implications for holistic health and well-being, reminding us that nurturing both mind and body is essential for a balanced life.

Emotions are not just fleeting feelings; they manifest as tangible physiological changes in our bodies. When you're anxious, for example, you might notice your heart racing, your palms sweating, or your muscles tensing up. This isn't a coincidence. The body responds to emotional stimuli with real, measurable changes. The autonomic nervous system (ANS) plays a critical role here, controlling involuntary bodily functions like heart rate and digestion. Emotions like stress and anxiety can activate the sympathetic nervous system, part of the ANS, leading to what's commonly known as the "fight or flight" response (Sapolsky, 2004).

Conversely, when you experience joy or contentment, your body shifts gears, often activating the parasympathetic nervous system, which is responsible for 'rest and digest' activities. This can result in a decrease in heart rate, muscle relaxation, and a general sense of calm (Porges, 2009). Embracing positive emotions not only enhances our immediate mood but can also bolster our long-term health, proving that our emotional landscape is etched into our physical form.

Scientific studies have found that emotions can influence inflammation levels in the body, a key factor in many chronic diseases. For instance, chronic stress and negative emotions have been associated with increased inflammation, which can contribute to conditions like cardiovascular disease, diabetes, and even cancer (Cohen et al., 2012). These findings underscore the importance of emotional regulation not just for mental health but as a cornerstone for physical health.

Understanding the influence of emotions on our physiology can empower us to take charge of our health. One practical approach is mindfulness, the process of maintaining a moment-by-moment awareness of our thoughts, feelings, bodily sensations, and the surrounding environment. Mindfulness practices, like meditation and yoga, have been shown to reduce stress and inflammation, thus fostering not only mental clarity but also physical well-being (Kabat-Zinn, 1990).

The healing potential of positive emotions is not just a theory; it's evidenced by the role of the placebo effect in medicine. Patients who believe they are receiving treatment often experience real physiological improvements, even when the "treatment" is nothing more than a sugar pill. This phenomenon highlights the body's remarkable ability to align with the mind's expectations, emphasizing the power of positive belief and emotion in physical healing (Benedetti, 2014).

Emotion-driven physiological responses aren't limited to stressful situations; they occur in a myriad of contexts. Consider how excitement or anticipation over a joyous occasion can lead to an elevated heart rate or "butterflies" in the stomach. These responses demonstrate the bidirectional flow of influence between emotions and physical reactions. Recognizing these patterns can help individuals anticipate and manage their emotional and physical responses to various situations, enhancing overall well-being.

The field of psychoneuroimmunology explores how emotional states can influence immune function. Studies show that positive emotions enhance immune responses, while negative emotions can suppress it. This implies that maintaining emotional balance can be crucial in defending the body against illnesses (Ader et al., 1987). Thus, cultivating emotional intelligence and resilience becomes not just a psychological advantage but a physiological one as well.

Cultivating positive emotions doesn't mean avoiding negative ones; rather, it involves processing and learning from all emotions constructively. Emotions are signals that provide insight into our experiences and ourselves. When recognized and addressed effectively, they can be powerful guides toward growth and healing. Embracing this intentional attention to emotions can lead to increased body-mind harmony (Gross, 1998).

The evidence is clear: emotions are not merely abstract states to be managed; they are significant determinants of physiological health. Recognizing and harnessing this interplay opens up a new realm of possibilities for enhancing both mental and physical well-being. By understanding how our emotions shape our physiology, we gain insight into the holistic synergy that underpins our health.

As we continue to explore the fascinating science behind this synchrony, it's vital to remember that the journey toward emotional and physical balance is personal and ongoing. The tools and insights gained here can be applied in everyday life, encouraging us to listen more intently to our bodies and emotions. In doing so, we create a harmonious path toward holistic health, one that honors both the mind and the body.

Chapter 3: Nourishing the Body, Nourishing the Mind

Nourishing your body is not just about filling your stomach; it's a profound act of feeding your mind and soul. The intricate dance between nutrition and mental wellness has been a focus of numerous studies, emphasizing that what we consume has a direct impact on how we think and feel. When you choose foods rich in essential nutrients, like omega-3 fatty acids, antioxidants, and vitamins, you're essentially giving your brain the fuel it needs to function optimally and combat cognitive decline (Gómez-Pinilla, 2008). This deep connection suggests that a balanced diet, abundant in fruits, vegetables, whole grains, and lean proteins, plays a crucial role in not only physical health but also mental clarity and emotional balance. Feeding the body with mindful awareness can transform eating into a meditation, where every bite is an acknowledgment of the symbiotic bond between body and mind. This holistic approach nurtures a harmonious internal environment, where health thrives on the macro and micro levels—physically manifesting as vitality and mentally as resilience. As you embrace this integrative nourishment, you don't just aim to survive but to excel and flourish in every aspect of life.

The Role of Nutrition in Mental Wellness

Embarking on the journey of nourishment transcends the physical realm, as what we consume profoundly influences our mental wellness.

Imagine your nutritional choices as the brushstrokes that paint the mind's landscape. A diet rich in essential nutrients like omega-3 fatty acids, vitamins, minerals, and antioxidants acts as a catalyst for optimal brain function and emotional balance. Scientific research has demonstrated the pivotal role of nutrition in mental health, evidencing how deficiencies in key nutrients can lead to mood disorders and cognitive decline (Marx et al., 2022). Importantly, gut health is also intertwined with mental wellness through the intricate brain-gut axis, where a well-balanced diet helps maintain this delicate harmony and supports serotonin production, a vital neurotransmitter involved in mood regulation (Mayer, 2019). As we prioritize nutrient-dense foods, we empower ourselves to think more clearly, manage stress more effectively, and embrace a more resilient state of being, creating a holistic integration of body and mind.

Brain Foods: What to Eat for a Healthy Mind finds its foundation in the understanding that our nutrition greatly impacts mental wellness. Picture nutrition as the bridge nurturing the vital connection between body and mind. Our diet's influence on mental clarity, cognitive function, and emotional stability is profound. Nutrients travel through the bloodstream, crossing the blood-brain barrier, each playing an intricate role in brain function. But what exactly should grace our plates to support optimal mental health?

Consider omega-3 fatty acids—the champions of brain nutrition. These essential fats, found abundantly in fatty fish like salmon, sardines, and mackerel, are known to improve cognitive functions and ward off depression (Grosso et al., 2014). The brain itself thrives on fat; approximately 60% of its mass is fatty tissue, making the intake of good fats crucial. Omega-3s have been shown to influence synaptic plasticity and neurotransmission, potentially enhancing learning and memory (McNamara, 2015).

Beyond fats, complex carbohydrates play a pivotal role in sustaining mental energy. They serve as the brain's primary source of fuel, breaking down into glucose, which powers neurons. Whole grains such as oats, barley, and quinoa deliver a slow and steady release of glucose. Unlike simple carbohydrates that lead to sudden spikes in blood sugar, whole grains provide sustained energy, preventing mood fluctuations (Benton, 2002).

Then there's the vibrant profile of antioxidants, found in fruits and vegetables of varied colors. Berries, like blueberries and strawberries, are particularly celebrated for their high levels of flavonoids—a type of antioxidant linked to cognitive performance. These compounds combat oxidative stress and inflammation, which can impede brain function (Spencer et al., 2012). A colorful diet ensures a rich supply of these protective nutrients, benefiting both brain health and spirit.

For those seeking to fortify mental resilience, consider the humble folate. This B-vitamin, abundant in leafy greens, citrus fruits, and legumes, is crucial for the synthesis of dopamine and serotonin—neurotransmitters foundational to mood regulation (Gilbody et al., 2007). A folate-rich diet has been linked to decreased risk of depression, bringing a lightness to the mind.

Let's not forget about hydration—often overlooked but critical for mental acuity. The brain is composed of nearly 75% water. Even mild dehydration can impact attentiveness, short-term memory, and concentration. Drinking adequate fluids keeps cognitive gears well-oiled, enabling smooth neural communication (Adan, 2012).

Diving deeper, probiotics found in fermented foods like yogurt, kefir, and sauerkraut light the path to mental clarity. The gut-brain axis, a key player in mental wellness, is bridged by a healthy microbiome. Fermented foods bolster gut health, influencing the production of neurotransmitters and aiding in reducing anxiety and depression symptoms (Kato-Kataoka et al., 2016).

A balanced diet isn't just about what you eat but also about what you avoid. Reducing processed foods, high in sugars and unhealthy fats, is critical. These foods may lead to inflammation and oxidative stress, hampering mental functions and increasing the risk of mood disorders (Jacka et al., 2010).

Caffeine, a familiar companion in the form of coffee and tea, deserves mention. While moderate consumption can enhance alertness and mood by blocking adenosine—a neurotransmitter that promotes sleepiness—excessive intake may lead to anxiety and disrupted sleep (Smith, 2002). Striking the right balance is imperative.

In the labyrinth of nutrition, individual needs vary. It's important to listen to one's body and adjust dietary practices according to its responses. What works for one may not suit another; personalization is key. Consulting with a healthcare professional or nutritionist can guide the creation of a customized brain-friendly menu.

Ultimately, nourishing the brain is about embracing a lifestyle of mindful eating. Intention, balance, and variety lay the groundwork for a well-functioning mind. Let food be a source of joy and vitality, guiding us toward a harmonious existence where body and mind thrive as one.

Creating a Balanced Diet for Physical and Mental Health

When we think about diet, we often focus on physical health, envisioning nutritious foods that strengthen our bodies. Yet, the ripple effect of our dietary choices extends far beyond muscle and bone. The food we consume plays a crucial role in mental wellness, impacting everything from our mood to our cognitive function. It's a symphony of nutrients working together, each note contributing to an overall sense of balance and vitality. To approach this harmony, one must consider both the science and the art of nourishment, and how what we eat can profoundly influence how we feel.

Understanding the connection between diet and mental health begins with recognizing that the brain is an energy-hungry organ. It requires a steady supply of nutrients to function optimally. Key nutrients such as omega-3 fatty acids, B vitamins, and antioxidants are vital players in brain health. Omega-3s, found in fatty fish like salmon, are well-known for their role in cognitive function and emotional regulation. Studies have linked adequate omega-3 intake to a reduced risk of depression and anxiety (Grosso et al., 2014). While supplements can offer a convenient source, incorporating these nutrients into our daily meals ensures a more balanced intake.

A balanced diet should also include adequate vitamins and minerals. Consider B vitamins, which are essential for brain function and energy production. Foods rich in complex carbohydrates such as whole grains, beans, and legumes provide a steady release of glucose, vital for sustaining energy levels. A consistent supply of glucose ensures that your brain has the fuel it needs, helping to stabilize mood and mental clarity. Similarly, vitamin D, often dubbed the "sunshine vitamin," has shown a potential relationship with mood disorders. Sunshine, moderate supplementation, and foods like fortified milk or orange juice contribute to maintaining optimal vitamin D levels (Brouwer-Brolsma et al., 2016).

In addition to macronutrients, the importance of micronutrients cannot be overstated. Zinc, magnesium, and iron also play significant roles in maintaining mental wellness. These minerals facilitate neurotransmitter functioning, which helps modulate mood and influence sleep patterns. A deficiency in any one of these can manifest in symptoms like irritability, depression, and cognitive dysfunction. It's essential to balance your intake of these nutrients through foods such as pumpkin seeds, nuts, and green leafy vegetables, ensuring that all bases are covered.

However, nutrition for mental and physical health isn't just about what you eat—it's about how you eat. Cultivating a mindful approach to eating can promote both mental clarity and emotional wellbeing. By paying attention to hunger signals, savoring each bite, and appreciating the flavors and textures of food, we can create a positive relationship with what nourishes us. Mindful eating not only enhances digestion but also bolsters our emotional satisfaction with meals, reducing tendencies toward overeating and compulsive eating habits.

Equally important is hydration; water is the fundamental element in almost all metabolic processes, including brain function. Dehydration can lead to confusion and mood swings. Consuming enough water helps maintain clarity and focus. Adding a squeeze of lemon or a handful of mint can make water more appealing, encouraging you to meet daily hydration needs effortlessly.

The gut-brain axis also deserves our attention. This bidirectional communication network between the gut and the brain means that what happens in the gut doesn't stay in the gut. Disruptions in gut microbiota have been linked to mental health issues such as depression and anxiety (Cryan & Dinan, 2012). Eating a diet rich in probiotics—like yogurt, kefir, and fermented foods—and prebiotics found in fiber-rich foods like bananas, onions, and garlic, helps in nurturing a healthy gut microbiome. This, in turn, supports mental health and resilience to stress.

As we strive for a diet that supports both our mental and physical wellbeing, balance remains key. This involves not only a variety of wholesome foods but also the occasional indulgence without guilt. A balanced approach encourages flexibility and sustainability, ensuring that our dietary habits can adapt to our body's changing needs over time. It's about creating a rhythm that acknowledges the nutritional complexity of foods and their multifaceted role in health.

In summary, nurturing physical and mental health through diet is a dynamic, integrative process. It demands an understanding of nutrition's impact on the body and mind, a thoughtful selection of foods that cater to our individual needs, and an appreciation for the enjoyment of eating. By making informed dietary choices, you're not just fueling a body; you're nurturing your mind and laying the foundation for a more fulfilling, energized life. As we continue to learn more about the powerful connection between nutrition and mental health, the potential for transformation is boundless.

Through scientific understanding and personal exploration, your journey toward a balanced diet can lead to new levels of vitality and emotional resilience. Start by listening to your body, honoring its needs, and respecting the wisdom that lies within your daily dietary choices. Together, let's embrace the food we eat as a true ally in living harmoniously within the interconnected web of body and mind.

Chapter 4: Movement as Medicine

Embracing the transformative power of movement offers a gateway to enhanced mental clarity and holistic health. Our bodies are designed to move, and when we honor this intrinsic need, we unlock a wealth of psychological benefits. Exercise, serving as a natural antidote to stress and anxiety, boosts endorphin production, which elevates mood and promotes mental clarity (Anderson & Shivakumar, 2013). Regular physical activity not only shapes our bodies but also nurtures our minds, creating a serene mental state that fosters resilience against life's challenges. Mindful movement practices such as yoga and tai chi blend the benefits of exercise with the calming effects of focused breathing, reinforcing the interconnectedness of our physical and mental states (Field, 2011). By integrating movement into our daily lives, we don't just build healthier bodies; we cultivate minds that are robust and ready to thrive amidst both calm and turbulence. The beauty of movement is that it doesn't demand perfection or an athlete's prowess; rather, it invites presence and awareness, urging each of us to find joy in the ebb and flow of physical expression. It transforms the act of moving from mere mechanics to a meditative, curative practice that attunes the body-mind connection.

The Psychological Effects of Exercise

Exercise is more than just a catalyst for physical fitness; it's a powerful promoter of psychological well-being. Engaging in regular physical activity triggers a cascade of positive mental effects, serving as a natural antidote to stress and anxiety. As the body moves, it releases endorphins and other neurotransmitters that interact with receptors in the brain to reduce the perception of pain and enhance mood, often described as the "runner's high" (Dishman et al., 2006). These neurochemical changes can lead to improved mood, greater sense of relaxation, and even a deeper connection to one's emotional state. In addition, consistent exercise fosters enhanced brain plasticity, improving cognitive functions such as memory and concentration (Ratey & Loehr, 2011). By integrating movement into daily life, individuals can unlock a sense of empowerment and resilience, creating a harmonious synergy between mind and body. This relationship underscores the profound impact of exercise as a form of medicine, extending beyond the physical to enrich the totality of our well-being.

Endorphins and Anxiety: Running Toward Mental Clarity

Embarking on a journey of self-discovery often means confronting the myriad of emotions that swirl within us. Among these emotions, anxiety can be a formidable force. It's no secret that modern life, with its relentless pace and constant demands, can stir up feelings of anxiety. However, nestled within the art of movement lies a powerful antidote: endorphins. As we dive deeper into this transformative chemical reaction, we'll explore how exercise, particularly running, can lead us to mental clarity.

Endorphins are neurotransmitters produced in the brain that act as natural painkillers and mood elevators. During physical activity, these biochemical compounds are released, interacting with receptors in the brain to reduce our perception of pain and act as a buffer against anxiety (Harber et al., 2011). Imagine them as nature's own mood-enhancing elixir, enhancing our capacity to cope with stressors.

Anxiety often manifests as a web of worrisome thoughts, excessive rumination, and a pervasive feeling of unease. When we're caught in this web, it can feel like there's no escape. But physical exercise provides a way out, a path towards freedom. Running, in particular, has been shown to stimulate the release of endorphins substantially, creating what many runners describe as a "runner's high"—a state of euphoria accompanied by reduced anxiety and an increased sense of well-being (Yeung, 1996).

Time and again, scientific studies affirm the benefits of exercise on mental health. A pivotal study led by the University of Georgia found that regular physical activity can reduce anxiety symptoms as effectively as medication in some cases (Herring et al., 2010). By engaging in regular bouts of running, you're not just increasing your physical endurance; you're also strengthening your mind, fostering a resilience that can counterbalance the weight of anxiety.

Let's delve into why running serves as such a potent vehicle against anxiety. The rhythmic nature of running encourages a meditative state. Each stride, each breath becomes a mantra, drawing the mind's focus away from anxious thoughts and into the present moment. This shift in focus is akin to meditative practices that ground us in mindfulness, offering a mental reprieve and fostering a clearer state of awareness.

Moreover, running in natural environments adds another layer of benefit. The practice of eco-therapy, which involves engaging with nature to improve wellbeing, greatly complements the effect of endorphins. Being outdoors amidst natural beauty enhances our mood and calms our minds. Research in environmental psychology suggests that exposure to green spaces reduces anxiety and increases overall mental clarity (Bratman et al., 2015).

Let's not overlook the social dimension of exercise—running groups and clubs have sprouted in communities across the globe. These environments offer more than just physical benefits; they foster connection. Sharing the path with others fighting similar mental battles can significantly reduce feelings of isolation, a common factor exacerbating anxiety. Emotional support, camaraderie, and community form an invisible network of resilience, bolstered by the shared release of endorphins.

As we lace up our sneakers and hit the track, trail, or pavement, we engage in a transformative act of self-care. Running propels us physically, of course, but it also propels us mentally into a space clear of overwhelming thoughts. With each mile, endorphins perform their intrinsic magic, paving the way for mental clarity. The effects might not be immediate for everyone; persistence, however, will unveil the profound psychological benefits.

But how can we integrate running into our already busy lives? The key is starting small, setting achievable goals. Perhaps begin with a brisk walk that transitions into a jog, and gradually, those jogs will turn into runs. Consistency outweighs intensity; a steady weekly routine ultimately cultivates the benefits of both endorphins and anxiety reduction.

In our increasingly sedentary world, exercise acts as a cornerstone for managing anxiety. The American Psychological Association acknowledges exercise not just as a physical pursuit, but a psychological strategy (American Psychological Association, 2011). Incorporating running into your life doesn't require Olympic-level commitment—it asks only for openness to movement's potential to heal.

Finally, it's crucial to approach this journey with compassion. Some days will be easier than others. The rhythm of running mirrors life's rhythms—it fluctuates. What's important is the commitment to return to the path, knowing it's a step toward mental clarity. As you embrace movement, find encouragement in the fact that you're part of a larger movement—a collective pursuit of harmony between body and mind.

Incorporating Mindful Movement into Daily Life

In the cacophony of modern life, we often find ourselves moved along as if on a conveyor belt, perpetually busy yet detached from our own bodies. Mindful movement invites us to slow down and savor the experience of being in motion, transforming everyday activities into a nourishing practice for both the body and the mind. By infusing purpose into movement, the mundane evolves into the extraordinary—a vehicle for enhanced awareness and holistic wellbeing.

Mindful movement isn't tied to a specific activity; it's a philosophy that can be applied to various physical practices, ranging from yoga and tai chi to everyday tasks like walking or even doing the dishes. The essence lies in the quality of attention you bring to the act of moving. When you engage in mindful movement, you cultivate a deep presence that anchors you to the present moment, liberating you from the ruminations of the past and the anxieties of the future.

For many, yoga is the gateway to mindful movement. As one stretches, bends, and balances, the body's actions synchronize with the breath, leading to a meditative state where the chatter of the mind quiets. Research has shown that practicing yoga can significantly reduce stress, anxiety, and depression, thereby promoting emotional balance (Davidson et al., 2003). This mind-body harmony isn't limited to yoga alone; the same principles can be extended to any form of movement.

Imagine transforming your morning walk into a mindful practice. Instead of planning your day or checking notifications, focus on the sensation of each foot touching the ground, the rhythm of your breath, and the sounds around you. This act of being fully present enhances your sensory awareness and deepens your connection with the world, grounding your mind and enlivening your spirit.

When integrated into daily life, mindful movement can serve as a versatile tool for managing stress and enhancing resilience. Numerous studies support the psychological benefits of physical activity, including the release of endorphins—our body's natural mood elevators (Dishman et al., 2006). By fostering mindful engagement during exercise or movement, these benefits are often amplified, leading to improved self-regulation and coping skills.

Incorporating this practice into hectic lifestyles is not just feasible but essential. Start small by incorporating mindful breathing into simple exercises or stretches. As muscles flow through motions, whether it's a yoga pose or a gentle plié, maintain an intentional focus on your breath. This connection anchors you, allowing for a richer experience of the present and promoting an internal landscape of calmness and acceptance.

Even routine activities like cleaning or cooking can be transformed. Picture yourself chopping vegetables with deliberation, feeling each slice, and listening to the rhythm it creates. Such mindful attention shifts the activity from being a mere task to a practice of meditation in action, encouraging a sense of fulfillment and peace.

Furthermore, mindful movement nurtures the mind-body connection, highlighting the interdependence of physical and mental health. As you practice, you're not merely engaging in physical activity; you are tapping into a healing loop that can reduce inflammation and improve mental clarity (Black & Slavich, 2016). Thus, the more you practice, the more attuned you become to your own body's signals and needs, fostering physical awareness and emotional intelligence.

To truly embody mindful movement, consistency is key. Create a routine that resonates with you, balancing structure with flexibility. Reflect on activities that bring you joy and conjure a state of flow, and identify how they can be imbued with mindfulness. Whether it's a sunset stroll or dance, dedicating time to this practice can be a transformative antidote to a fast-paced life.

The journey of mindful movement isn't solely an individual pursuit. Engaging in group activities like tai chi or dance classes can amplify the experience through communal energy and shared intentions. Additionally, sharing this practice with others extends its benefits to a wider circle, fostering a sense of community and collective mindfulness.

In essence, incorporating mindful movement into daily life is not about a drastic overhaul but rather a gentle integration of awareness into the rhythm of your days. It's a call to live more fully and move more deliberately, finding beauty and tranquility in each motion, each breath. Through practice, the movement becomes a medicinal balm, soothing the mind, invigorating the body, and aligning them in harmonious concert.

As you embark on this journey, remember that mindfulness in movement is a practice, not a destination. Embrace it with curiosity and compassion, and allow its principles to unfold organically in your life. The benefits of such a practice—mental clarity, emotional resilience, and physical vitality—are waiting to be uncovered within each deliberate step.

By cultivating mindful movement, you're not just nurturing your physical health but crafting a sanctuary within yourself, a space where inner peace and strength coexist in harmony. The possibilities are boundless, and the journey uniquely yours, as you move through life with purpose and awareness.

Chapter 5: Mastering Stress Management

Stress isn't just a mental burden; it's a physiological reaction that can impact every cell in our body. Mastering stress management is not merely about reducing stress, but about transforming it into an ally that fuels growth and resilience. One of the key techniques involves harnessing the power of relaxation, from deep breathing exercises that activate the parasympathetic nervous system to progressive muscle relaxation, which reduces physical tension (McEwen & Stellar, 1993). Developing resilience is about adopting a mindset that sees stress as a challenge rather than a threat, empowering individuals to turn adversity into strength. Scientific studies suggest that resilience can buffer the detrimental effects of stress, thereby promoting both mental and physical health (Fletcher & Sarkar, 2013). By embracing these techniques, we can cultivate a balanced life, navigating the demands of modern living with grace and strength. Stress management is a dynamic process, an integral part of the lifelong journey toward holistic wellbeing.

Stress-Reduction Techniques That Really Work

Stress is an inevitable part of life, yet mastering effective reduction techniques is crucial for maintaining overall wellbeing. From deep breathing to progressive muscle relaxation, these science-backed methods foster a calmer and more resilient mind. Deep breathing, a cornerstone of many mindfulness practices, helps activate the parasympathetic nervous system, lowering heart rates and blood pressure (Jerath et al., 2015). Progressive muscle relaxation, on the other hand, involves tensing and then relaxing muscle groups, which can reduce tension and improve emotional regulation (McCallie et al., 2006). These practices don't just help manage stress; they encourage resilience, turning life's pressures into opportunities for growth. With consistent practice, anyone can cultivate a more tranquil and focused mind, enhancing both mental and physical health.

The Art of Relaxation: From Deep Breathing to Progressive Muscle Relaxation invites you to embark on a transformative journey. While it's easy to dismiss relaxation techniques as mere breaks from a hectic day, they are powerful tools for mastering stress management. When practiced consistently, these methods profoundly impact well-being by harmonizing the mind and body. Within this realm, deep breathing and progressive muscle relaxation stand out not only for their simplicity but for their scientific backing and effectiveness in reducing stress and enhancing mental health.

Deep breathing is more than just an act of inhaling and exhaling; it's a science-backed gateway to tranquility. This technique has roots in ancient practices and is often a fundamental part of disciplines like yoga and tai chi. When we take slow, deep breaths, we activate the parasympathetic nervous system — the part responsible for rest and digestion. This activation can slow the heartbeat, lower blood pressure, and decrease the body's cortisol levels, all of which are markers of stress reduction (Jerath et al., 2006).

One of the most accessible forms of deep breathing is diaphragmatic breathing, where you focus on inhaling deeply into your diaphragm rather than shallowly into your chest. This method engages the full capacity of your lungs, promoting more oxygen exchange. Such oxygenation is believed to foster a sense of mental clarity and relaxation, making it an invaluable tool for those dealing with anxiety or high-pressure environments (Zaccaro et al., 2018). The beauty of diaphragmatic breathing is that it can be practiced anywhere, anytime, requiring nothing more than a willingness to pause and breathe deeply.

Progressive Muscle Relaxation (PMR), on the other hand, is a technique that gently leads you through a cycle of tension and release. Developed by Dr. Edmund Jacobson in the 1930s, PMR is built on the concept that physical relaxation can lead to mental calmness. It involves systematically tensing and then relaxing different muscle groups, starting from the toes and progressing to the scalp. This focused attention on specific muscles interrupts the cycle of stress by providing a contrasting physical experience of relaxation that the mind can follow.

Practicing PMR isn't just about physical relaxation. It's also a mental exercise that teaches awareness of tension and how to let it go. Often, we aren't even aware of the knots of tension we hold until we deliberately focus on individual muscles. By regularly engaging in PMR, individuals can train themselves to notice and short-circuit muscle tension before it escalates into stress symptoms like headaches or back pain (McCallie et al., 2006).

As you begin integrating these techniques into your life, it's essential to approach them not as isolated practices but as integral parts of a larger stress-management strategy. Each method complements the other — with deep breathing serving as a quick intervention for immediate stressors, while PMR becomes a scheduled ritual for deeper relaxation and self-awareness. When combined, they create a robust toolset for reducing stress and achieving a balanced state of mind

Inhaling peace and exhaling tension through deep breathing, and the gradual loosening up through PMR, might seem like simple acts. However, their impact on the mind-body connection is profound. These techniques teach us awareness and control over our physiological responses to stress. With practice, we can cultivate a steady mind even in the stormiest circumstances. This balance doesn't just improve mental health; it roots us in a more resilient and adaptable physical state.

The process of relaxation is both an art and a science — it requires the creativity to tailor practices to one's lifestyle and the consistency to make them habitual. For those ready to embark on this journey, consider starting by setting aside a few minutes each day to practice deep breathing or PMR. These practices, while beneficial in silence, can also be enhanced with guided audio from mindfulness apps or soothing music that resonates with your personal rhythm.

Moreover, as you continue to progress, reflect on the subtle changes within your mind and body. Are the daily stressors fading more into the background? Is there a newfound sense of poise in your reactions? These are signs of a blossoming relaxation practice. Understanding that mastery takes time, gently encourage yourself with appreciation for each moment spent in dedication to your well-being.

Incorporating these relaxation techniques into your routine isn't about driving immediate changes but is instead akin to a gardener watering plants — with patience, nurturing, and care. Over time, you'll find that tranquility becomes an intrinsic part of your being, blossoming naturally in your everyday experiences. Whether you're a wellness enthusiast, healthcare professional seeking integrative approaches, or anyone eager for personal development, embracing these practices can guide you toward a balanced and harmonious life.

As you cultivate these skills, remember the power of community. Joining groups or classes that focus on relaxation techniques can enhance your practice, offering shared wisdom and encouragement. Learning from and with others can magnify your understanding and appreciation of the art of relaxation.

Ultimately, the pursuit of relaxation and stress management isn't just about reducing stress but about unlocking the potential within every aspect of your life. By committing to these simple yet profound practices, you harness the art of relaxation — transforming stress into strength and turbulence into tranquility. May this journey bring you peace, presence, and the profound harmony you seek.

Building Resilience: Turning Stress Into Strength

Resilience isn't just a trait you either have or you don't; it's a skill you can cultivate. In the face of stress, resilience transforms life's inevitable challenges into opportunities for growth. When stress hits, whether from a demanding work project or personal upheavals, resilient individuals don't just survive—they thrive. It's like turning the pain of lifting weights into muscle strength, only this time it's about fortifying your mental muscles. What does it mean to turn stress into strength? Simply put, it's the art of building resilience.

The body reacts to stress through the release of hormones such as adrenaline and cortisol. This physiological response, known as the 'fight or flight' mechanism, is crucial for survival but can be corrosive if activated continuously. The key to combating this cycle is understanding that stress isn't entirely detrimental; in moderation, it can serve as a catalyst for growth. This perspective shift is often the first step toward harnessing stress constructively. Your challenge is to learn how to manage and utilize this physiological reaction to bolster, rather than diminish, your life (McEwen, 2017).

Certainly, resilience draws heavily on emotional intelligence—our ability to recognize, understand, and manage our emotions. Resilient people are emotionally attuned. They recognize triggers and early signs of stress, allowing them to take proactive steps rather than react impulsively. The ability to stay calm under pressure is tied closely to self-awareness and emotional regulation strategies. By practicing mindfulness, individuals can enhance their emotional intelligence, allowing them to tackle life's challenges with greater poise and composure.

Resilience also involves cognitive restructuring techniques, such as reframing negative thoughts. An effective way to foster resilience is to train the mind towards optimism. This isn't about ignoring problems but rather adopting a glass-half-full mindset. For instance, viewing a challenging situation as a learning opportunity rather than a setback can significantly alter its impact. Cognitive Behavioral Therapy (CBT) often adopts this approach to help patients develop healthier thinking patterns that lead to improved emotional well-being (Beck, 2011).

Building social support systems is another powerful resilience-building strategy. Humans are inherently social creatures, and meaningful social connections offer profound strength. They provide not only practical aid but emotional support, offering different perspectives and reminding us we're not alone in our struggles. Strong social networks can buffer against stress, making adversities appear less daunting. This is perhaps why community and connection, as noted in the later chapters, are essential components of health and well-being.

Resilience training isn't complete without addressing the physical aspect. Regular physical activity can't be overstated. Not only is exercise beneficial for physical health, but it also serves as a powerful stress release and increases resilience. Exercise reduces anxiety, depression, and, crucially, stress levels, as it prompts the release of endorphins—natural mood lifters that create feelings of happiness and euphoria. Even a simple daily walk can significantly impact stress levels, promoting resilience (Erickson et al., 2015).

Additionally, resilience thrives on flexibility—both mental and physical. This flexibility means being open to change and willing to adjust plans as necessary rather than rigidly sticking to a predetermined path. Cultivating a flexible mindset helps in navigating uncertainty with creativity and innovation rather than fear and rigidity. Yoga, for instance, not only improves physical flexibility but also encourages a state of mental pliability by merging movement with mindfulness.

Just as importantly, resilience builds over time through self-compassion. Often, when you're hit by failure or tough times, the inner critic reawakens, exacerbating stress. Self-compassion encourages a kinder inner dialogue. Rather than berating oneself for perceived inadequacies, resilient individuals practice forgiving themselves and seeing these moments as part of the human experience. By recognizing that everyone stumbles, a sense of connectedness replaces isolation, fostering emotional resilience.

Resilience also means being able to bounce back from failures and learn from life's lessons. Embracing a growth mindset—the belief that abilities and intelligence can be developed through effort—can be transformative. Approaching life with curiosity and a willingness to learn from experience enables you to evolve with each challenge. Progress, not perfection, is the goal, and even setbacks are valuable teachers.

Finally, it's essential to embrace relaxation techniques that support stress management. Complementary practices such as progressive muscle relaxation and meditation have long shown promise in reducing stress and enhancing resilience. These practices train the mind and body to achieve a state of calm, even in the midst of chaos, creating a fertile ground for resilience to flourish.

As we navigate through an increasingly complex world, the construction of resilience could not be more relevant. It's not merely about weathering the storm but learning how to dance in the rain. As we master stress management, turning stress into strength becomes our most valuable tool, enabling us to lead lives that are not only fulfilling but robust.

Chapter 6:
The Art and Science of Sleep

Sleep, often considered a passive state, is a dynamic and complex process integral to our physical and mental well-being. It's not just about closing our eyes and drifting off; it's a wondrous balance of art and science that rejuvenates the brain, consolidates memories, and regulates emotions. Scientific studies underscore the essential role sleep plays in mental health, suggesting that poor sleep can lead to anxiety, depression, and a disruption in our body's ability to manage stress (Walker & Stickgold, 2019). On an experiential level, cultivating sleep hygiene practices—like maintaining a consistent sleep schedule and optimizing our sleep environment—can transform our nights into a sanctuary for restoration (Hirshkowitz et al., 2015). Moreover, understanding the biological processes involved in sleep, such as the interplay between circadian rhythms and homeostatic sleep drive, equips us with the tools to nurture this vital aspect of our health. In the hands of those embracing holistic well-being, sleep becomes not just a nightly ritual but a conscious and empowering choice towards a harmonious body-mind connection.

Understanding Sleep's Role in Mental Health

Sleep is often the unsung hero in the pursuit of mental wellbeing, serving as a foundational pillar that supports our emotional and psychological landscapes. Scientific research consistently underscores the necessity of quality sleep in regulating mood, cognitive function, and emotional resilience (Walker, 2017). When we sleep, our brains undergo crucial processes such as memory consolidation and emotional processing, which help us respond more adaptively to stressors in our waking lives (Rasch & Born, 2013). Lack of proper rest can contribute to difficulties in emotional regulation and increases the risk of mental health issues like anxiety and depression (Baglioni et al., 2011). In a world abuzz with relentless activity, cultivating an environment conducive to restorative sleep is no longer just an option but an essential ingredient for nurturing our body-mind harmony. Investing in structured sleep hygiene practices not only revitalizes our physical self but also empowers our mental fortitude, paving the way for a balanced and vibrant life.

Sleep Hygiene: Best Practices for Restorative Sleep emerges as a critical focus within our ongoing exploration of the body-mind connection. Within the realm of "Understanding Sleep's Role in Mental Health," it is essential to recognize the profound impact sleep has on our mental well-being. Just as nutrition and exercise form the foundation of physical health, sleep hygiene provides the necessary groundwork for mental clarity and emotional resilience. The principles of sleep hygiene are akin to a finely tuned instrument: when cared for with precision, it produces harmony in our mental health.

We are all aware that sleep is crucial, yet many overlook its potent influence on our mental health. Good sleep hygiene is not just about getting enough hours of rest but rather ensuring the quality of that rest is restorative. This revolves around adopting specific behaviors and creating an environment conducive to sleep, thus setting the stage for improved mental health. Research continually highlights the bidirectional nature of the relationship between sleep and mental health. Poor sleep can exacerbate mental health disorders, and mental health disorders can lead to poor sleep (Harvey et al., 2011).

Understanding sleep's essential role requires a closer look at our daily habits. We don't often consider how much our routines during the day influence our nights. Engaging in regular physical activity, managing stress effectively, and consuming a nutritious diet significantly affect our sleep quality. For instance, exercise boosts endorphins, which can enhance mood and promote better sleep, while a balanced diet provides the nutrients your body needs to maintain optimal function.

Moreover, winding down before bed and establishing a routine cues our mind and body that it's time to sleep. This can involve simple practices like dimming the lights, reducing screen time, or engaging in gentle stretching and meditation. Such practices cultivate a serene atmosphere, signaling to our nervous system that it is safe to enter a restorative state. A study by de Almondes and Leonardo (2010) revealed that consistent pre-sleep routines significantly improved sleep quality in participants.

Creating a sleep-conducive environment is paramount to proper sleep hygiene. Our bedrooms should be sanctuaries of rest, free from disturbances that might interrupt our sleep. Factors such as room temperature, noise levels, and bedding quality are essential components. A comfortable mattress and supportive pillows can make a difference, just as choosing the right room temperature can help you circulate fresh air. Keeping electronic devices out of the bedroom minimizes disruptive stimuli, allowing the brain to switch off more effectively.

Examining the impact of light exposure sheds light on the influence of modern lifestyles on our sleep cycles. Artificial light, particularly blue light from screens, can disrupt our circadian rhythms by interfering with the production of melatonin, the hormone that regulates sleep. Limiting screen time in the evening has been shown to support more rapid onset of sleep and improved sleep quality (Chang et al., 2015). Establishing boundaries with technology isn't just about cutting out distractions—it's about honoring our body's natural rhythm.

Yet, beyond the tangible changes we can make, the core of sleep hygiene also lies in listening to our bodies and acknowledging the signals that it sends us. There's wisdom in understanding when fatigue sets in and responding accordingly. This mindfulness towards our sleep needs opens pathways to cultivating better mental health. Embracing sleep as an ally rather than a nightly interruption to our day shifts our perception and encourages a healthier relationship with rest.

In weaving together the threads of sleep hygiene, the integrative perspective invites us to align our habits with our mental health goals. We are called to see beyond immediate comfort and prioritize practices that serve long-term well-being. Mental health benefits not only from deep, healthy sleep but from the intention that precedes it. It's an art form, one that requires patience and dedication, yet rewards us with a clearer vision of our emotional selves.

Finally, remember that sleep hygiene isn't about achieving perfection. It's an evolving practice that requires attention and respect for one's individual needs. Reflect on what's working and be open to change. As you deepen your understanding of the entwined nature of sleep and mental well-being, you'll find empowerment in these practices, enabling a more harmonious balance in your life.

Incorporate these sleep hygiene practices mindfully, and allow the serene support of restful nights to foster resilience and emotional stability. After all, restorative sleep forms the cornerstone of a vibrant mind, and it's well within our grasp. By nurturing our sleep environment and habits, we cultivate not only the art of sleep but the dance of life with greater ease and grace.

Creating a Sleep-Conducive Environment

In the intricate dance of our daily lives, sleep stands as a pillar of rejuvenation, crucial for maintaining the delicate balance between mind and body. To truly unlock sleep's restorative power, it's essential to delve into the art of designing an environment that's inherently conducive to rest. A harmonious sleep setting isn't just about comfort; it's about aligning our surroundings with our biological rhythms and psychological needs.

A bedroom that fosters sleep begins with the notion of sanctuary. Our sleep space should be a haven, free from the chaos and clutter that characterize our waking hours. Decluttering the bedroom helps to calm the mind, signaling that it's time to wind down. Studies have shown that visual distractions can raise stress levels, making it harder to drift into the restful state required for quality sleep (Smith et al., 2019).

Lighting plays a pivotal role in setting the stage for restful sleep. Natural cycles of light and dark were the original cues that governed human sleep patterns, and emulating these cycles can be deeply beneficial. Dim, warm lighting in the evening assists in the production of melatonin, the hormone responsible for regulating sleep-wake cycles (Cajochen et al., 2019). Conversely, exposure to blue light, often emitted by phones and computers, can disrupt these cycles, delaying the onset of sleep (Chang et al., 2015). Investing in blackout curtains or an eye mask can be instrumental in limiting unwanted light exposure.

Temperature control is another vital factor in crafting the ideal sleep environment. Cooler room temperatures, typically around 60 to 67 degrees Fahrenheit, are generally recommended for optimal sleep (Okamoto-Mizuno & Mizuno, 2012). Our core body temperature naturally decreases during the night, and a cooler room helps to facilitate this process. Bedding should be breathable and comfortable, further aiding in temperature regulation to prevent any disturbances in the night.

Noises from the external world can intrude upon the sanctuary of sleep. Soundproofing a bedroom, though potentially costly, can significantly enhance sleep quality for those living in noisy environments. Simple solutions, such as a fan or a white noise machine, can mask intrusive noises, helping to maintain the tranquility needed for uninterrupted sleep.

Fragrance, often overlooked, can play a subtle but important role in creating a sleep-conducive atmosphere. Aromatherapy, using scents like lavender and chamomile, has been shown to enhance relaxation and promote deeper sleep (Goel et al., 2005). Using essential oil diffusers or pillow sprays can help incorporate these calming scents into your nightly routine.

Consideration of electromagnetic radiation is a newer facet of optimizing sleep environments. Limiting exposure to electronic devices not only reduces blue light but also potential sources of electromagnetic fields (EMFs). Some individuals find that distancing electronic devices from the sleep space reduces disturbances, although scientific consensus on this is still emerging (Halgamuge, 2017).

The psychological impact of sleep environment aesthetics shouldn't be underestimated. Choosing calming colors and fabrics, investing in ergonomic furniture, and personalizing the space with cherished items can contribute to a sense of wellbeing and belonging. These elements create a serene backdrop that can soothe an active mind and make the transition to sleep more seamless.

Transforming your bedroom into a sleep haven doesn't require an overhaul; even small changes can make a significant difference. Start with simplicity and build from there, understanding that it's a personal journey. What works for one may not work for another, and experimentation is key. By tailoring your environment to your specific needs, you can foster a space that nurtures restorative sleep—allowing both body and mind to wake rejuvenated, ready to meet the challenges of a new day.

Chapter 7: Mindfulness and Meditation

Mindfulness and meditation serve as bridges connecting the realms of mental tranquility and physical vitality, offering profound avenues for enhancing wellbeing. These practices draw upon ancient wisdom and modern science to cultivate a deeper awareness of our thoughts, emotions, and bodily sensations, thereby fostering a harmony that transcends the stress and chaos of daily life. By focusing on the present moment with intentionality and openness, mindfulness enhances our ability to respond to life's challenges with clarity and composure, making it a powerful tool for mental and physical health (Kabat-Zinn, 2003). Meditation, on the other hand, offers a sanctuary for the mind, allowing it to reach a state of restful alertness that promotes cognitive resilience and emotional balance (Goyal et al., 2014). Whether through guided meditations, mindful breathing, or body awareness techniques, these practices equip individuals with practical strategies to navigate the complexities of modern existence, reinforcing the interconnectedness of the mind and body (Shapiro et al., 2006). This chapter delves into the art of mindfulness and meditation, exploring diverse styles and their distinct benefits, while offering practical insights for seamlessly integrating them into the tapestry of everyday life.

Cultivating Awareness for Mental and Physical Health

In the realm of mindfulness and meditation, cultivating awareness is essential for nurturing both mental and physical health. Awareness acts as a bridge, linking the mind and body, fostering a vital state of presence where one can more effectively manage stress and gain clarity (Kabat-Zinn, 1990). By becoming attuned to the nuances of our internal and external environments through practices such as mindful breathing and body scans, we're not only improving mental resilience but also enhancing physical well-being. Scientific research has demonstrated that consistent mindfulness practices can lead to significant changes in brain regions associated with attention, self-regulation, and empathy, thereby promoting a holistic sense of balance and calm (Tang et al., 2015; Goyal et al., 2014). This heightened awareness doesn't just help us face life's challenges with equanimity—it empowers us to make conscious choices that support our overall health and happiness. As you integrate these practices into your daily life, remember that each moment of awareness is a step towards a deeper, more fulfilling connection with yourself.

Different Styles of Meditation and Their Benefits meditators, old and new alike, often find themselves exploring a variety of meditation styles to harmonize their mental and physical health. While the overarching goal of meditation—to cultivate awareness and achieve a state of calm and clarity—maintains a common thread across different styles, each method offers unique benefits. These variations cater to individual needs, whether one seeks to reduce stress, enhance focus, or deepen self-awareness.

One popular style of meditation is Mindfulness Meditation, rooted in Buddhist practices. It involves paying attention to thoughts, emotions, and physical sensations in a nonjudgmental way. By fostering a state of presence without attachment, practitioners often find a reduction in stress and an improvement in emotional regulation. According to Kabat-Zinn (2003), mindfulness can enhance concentration and increase one's resilience to external stressors, making it a valuable tool for managing both mental and physiological health challenges.

Transcendental Meditation (TM) offers a different approach, designed to allow the mind to settle effortlessly into a state of profound rest. Practiced by silently repeating a mantra, TM has been associated with significant reductions in blood pressure and anxiety (Rosenthal, 2012). Researchers have found that regular practitioners of TM experience improved cardiovascular health, contributing to a holistic state of well-being that permeates both body and mind (Eppley et al., 1989).

For those who thrive on movement over stillness, Walking Meditation provides an excellent alternative. Often associated with Zen Buddhism, this practice involves walking slowly while maintaining awareness of each step and breath. This form of meditation can be particularly appealing for individuals who find it challenging to sit still for extended periods. Furthermore, walking meditation provides the added benefit of gentle physical exercise, which supports cardiovascular health and enhances mental clarity (Teasdale et al., 2000).

In contrast, Loving-Kindness Meditation (also known as Metta) cultivates an attitude of unconditional love and compassion towards oneself and others. This practice involves silently repeating phrases of goodwill and gradually extending that kindness from oneself to loved ones, then broader circles of people. Research has shown that Loving-Kindness Meditation can increase positive emotions and social connectedness, contributing to improved psychological health (Fredrickson et al., 2008). It acts as a balm not only for the mind but also promotes a nurturing bond with others, which can profoundly support emotional and physical healing.

Body Scan Meditation invites practitioners to focus attention sequentially on different parts of the body. This technique can deepen bodily awareness and promote relaxation, facilitating the release of tension and stress (Carmody & Baer, 2008). Regular practice of body scan meditation is associated with increased somatic awareness, which enhances the body-mind connection and can lead to more intuitive self-care decisions in daily life.

Additionally, Guided Visualization is a meditation style that uses mental imagery to foster relaxation and alter perceptions positively. By visualizing specific scenes or outcomes, practitioners can unlock creativity and positively influence their physical state by reducing stress hormones (Zeidan et al., 2010). Visualization allows individuals to mentally rehearse success and wellness, forging new neural pathways that align their thoughts with their aspirations.

The use of Meditation Apps has gained traction, offering various styles and guided sessions to suit contemporary lifestyles. Apps provide accessibility and can support a daily meditation practice through structured guidance and community features. While some purists might argue against technology-assisted meditation, these tools offer a gateway to mindfulness and a personalized meditation routine that can be particularly beneficial for those who struggle with consistency.

On a communal level, Group Meditation brings a collective energy that can enhance individual experiences. Participating in group meditation offers shared support, a sense of community, and accountability, which can enhance the depth of one's practice. The collective resonance of group energy is known to amplify intentions and accelerate personal growth, offering insights that may otherwise remain dormant (Reis et al., 2000).

The benefits of different meditation styles are as diverse as the individuals who practice them. While each method has its own merits, all contribute to cultivating a heightened state of awareness and interconnectedness within oneself and, paradoxically, with the wider world. Whether the path is stillness or movement, directed attention or open awareness, meditation remains a profound tool for enhancing total body-mind wellness—an avenue towards a more balanced and fulfilled life.

In a world that often feels disjointed, integrating meditation into daily life serves as both a refuge and a lens through which to view the world with greater clarity and compassion. As scientific research continues to affirm, the diverse practices of meditation contribute to the symphony of life, allowing us to harmonize the cacophony of modern existence into a melody of peace and possibility.

Practical Applications of Mindfulness in Daily Life

Mindfulness isn't just a theoretical concept reserved solely for monks on mountaintops or yogis in serene studios. It's a transformative practice that can seamlessly integrate into the busy fabric of our daily lives. By nurturing a state of present-moment awareness, mindfulness helps cultivate a profound sense of presence and interconnectedness, enhancing both mental and physical health.

Consider the simple act of eating. Often, meals are consumed hurriedly, driven by the day's chaos and an insatiable pace. Yet, the act of mindful eating transforms each meal into an opportunity for meditation. When we pay attention to the textures, flavors, and aromas, and recognize our body's hunger and satiety cues, we engage in a deeper dialogue with our bodies. This practice not only enhances digestion but can also foster a healthier relationship with food. Scientific literature supports this, highlighting benefits like reduced binge eating and improved emotional regulation associated with mindful eating (Kristeller & Wolever, 2011).

Mindful walking is another practice that invites mindfulness into the folds of daily life. Amidst urban life's hustle and bustle, walking mostly feels like a means to an end. However, when approached mindfully, walking turns into a purposeful activity, inviting you to engage with your surroundings fully and appreciate the present moment. The rhythmic motion becomes a dance of balance and coordination, offering a meditative state where stress and anxiety fade. Studies indicate that mindful walking reduces depressive symptoms and increases body awareness, offering a dual benefit for mental and physical health (Teasdale et al., 2000).

We live in a world constantly vying for our attention—emails, notifications, and perpetual to-do lists. Mindful working provides a refuge amidst the storm of distractions. By focusing on one task at a time, employing deep breathing techniques to reset your focus, and setting intentional breaks to recalibrate, work becomes more than just ticking off tasks. It transforms into a meaningful activity, paving the way for increased productivity and reduced burnout. Research shows that mindfulness at work is linked to better employee engagement, increased job satisfaction, and reduced stress (Good et al., 2016).

The benefits of incorporating mindfulness into family routines can't be overstated. Families can practice together through simple rituals like gratitude exercises before meals or mindful breathing at the start and end of the day. These practices foster emotional intelligence and open communication, essential components for nurturing healthy relationships. Children, in particular, benefit from shared mindfulness exercises, which can enhance their focus, emotional regulation, and resilience in the face of life's challenges (Zelazo & Lyons, 2012).

Driving, an activity that often fuels stress and frustration, can also benefit from mindfulness. Mindful driving encourages focusing on the sensory experience of driving—the feel of the steering wheel, the hum of the engine, and the changing scenery. This heightened awareness not only enhances safety by reducing distraction-related incidents but also transforms the drive into a meditative experience, easing tension and promoting calm.

Consider also the integration of mindfulness in conversations. Mindful communication involves active listening, paying full attention without immediately formulating a response, and being fully present with the person you're speaking with. It's more than merely waiting for your turn to speak. This form of communication fosters deeper connections, reduces misunderstandings, and strengthens relationships, making interactions more meaningful and empathetic.

Household chores, mundane as they may seem, are ripe opportunities for mindfulness. By focusing on the task at hand, whether it's washing dishes or folding laundry, you enter a meditative state that emphasizes presence rather than the chore's completion. This shift in perspective transforms daily tasks from monotonous routines into meaningful practices that ground us in the present moment.

A growing body of research underscores the tangible benefits of mindfulness practices in managing chronic pain and fostering mental resilience. By grounding attention in the present, individuals report less pain intensity and a better quality of life (Kabat-Zinn, 1982). This powerful insight can transform the way individuals approach health challenges, highlighting mindfulness as an integral tool in a holistic health toolkit.

Incorporating mindfulness into exercise routines, like yoga or tai chi, offers additional advantages beyond physical fitness. These mindful movement practices blend physical activity with mental clarity, promoting an integrated approach to wellness that nurtures both the body and mind simultaneously.

Start small. Implement mindfulness in daily routines by identifying moments that can be mindfully altered. By anchoring mindfulness in these small acts, you open the door to a life enriched with peace, resilience, and clarity. Though challenges will inevitably arise, a mindful response builds the muscles of patience and acceptance, creating a fertile ground for personal growth and transformation.

Personal reflection on mindfulness practice is equally significant. Spend a few minutes each day reflecting on the moments when you successfully applied mindfulness and those when you fell short. This reflective practice not only measures progress but also reinforces mindfulness as a valued habit, paving the way for continued growth.

Through practical applications, mindfulness transcends its image as a solitary practice, weaving itself seamlessly into daily life. As you open yourself to mindfulness, you'll find a renewed sense of harmony and balance, creating a life that not only functions but flourishes. The journey toward mindfulness is deeply personal yet universally beneficial, extending its roots into all facets of life. Let mindfulness be the thread that weaves your daily existence into a tapestry of peace, presence, and purpose.

Chapter 8: Emotional Balance for Physical Wellbeing

In the delicate interweaving of body and mind, our emotional landscape profoundly influences our physical health. Emotional balance isn't just a lofty ideal; it's a vital element of our overall well-being. Harnessing this balance begins with recognizing that emotions can impact bodily systems like immunity and cardiovascular health, echoing through our physiology with surprising resonance (Kiecolt-Glaser et al., 2015). To nurture this harmony, it's crucial to develop strategies for managing emotions, which can range from mindfulness practices to cognitive reframing techniques (Gross, 2002). Embracing these methods not only fortifies mental health but also acts as a buffer against stress-related ailments, fostering resilience and healing from within. Psychosomatic medicine underscores this connection, highlighting how emotional well-being can stimulate physiological healing and vice versa, creating a feedback loop of health (Lakhan & Schofield, 2013). By cultivating emotional balance, we unlock a cascade of benefits, enhancing our vitality and paving the way for a life filled with energy and purpose.

The Impact of Mental Health on Disease and Immunity

Mental health isn't just a state of mind; it profoundly influences our physical health, particularly when it comes to disease and immunity. When we experience chronic stress or emotional turmoil, our bodies release stress hormones like cortisol, which over time can suppress immune function and leave us more vulnerable to infections and illnesses (Cohen et al., 2012). This connection underlines the intricate dance between our emotional and physical states, where mental health challenges can exacerbate physical symptoms, creating a cycle that's hard to break. Conversely, cultivating emotional balance through practices like mindfulness and meditation can foster resilience, reducing the release of harmful stress hormones and enhancing the immune system's capacity to fight off disease (Davidson & Kaszniak, 2015). By integrating mind and body practices into our daily routines, we not only nurture our mental and emotional health but also fortify our bodies against potential threats, paving the way for holistic well-being.

Strategies for Managing Emotions are key to maintaining the harmony between mind and body, especially when considering *The Impact of Mental Health on Disease and Immunity*. As we delve deeper into the body-mind connection, it becomes increasingly clear that emotions are not just abstract experiences but rather powerful influencers of physical health. Managing emotions effectively is an essential strategy for promoting overall wellbeing, particularly in safeguarding against diseases and fortifying the immune system.

Emotions such as stress, anger, or sadness can manifest not only in one's mood but also in various physiological changes that impact health. When chronic, these emotions can leave the body in a state of heightened arousal or prolonged stress, triggering the release of stress hormones like cortisol. Over time, this can weaken the immune system, making one more susceptible to illnesses and impairing the body's ability to heal (McEwen, 2006). Fortunately, there are practical strategies we can employ to manage these emotions, thus mitigating their negative effects on physical health.

One of the most effective strategies for emotional management is mindfulness meditation. By fostering a state of calm and awareness, mindfulness allows individuals to observe their thoughts and feelings without immediate reaction, reducing the impact of stress and anxiety (Goyal et al., 2014). Regular practice of mindfulness has been shown to decrease cortisol levels, thereby enhancing immune function and reducing the inflammation that often accompanies stress (Black & Slavich, 2016). Whether it's through meditation, mindful breathing, or simply pausing to truly engage in the present moment, mindfulness empowers individuals to regain control over their emotional responses.

Alongside mindfulness, cognitive-behavioral strategies offer another valuable approach. By recognizing and altering thought patterns that lead to negative emotional states, individuals can break the cycle of stress and negativity. Techniques such as cognitive restructuring help to identify irrational thoughts and replace them with more balanced perspectives, promoting a healthier emotional environment. Studies have shown that these strategies can reduce symptoms of anxiety and depression, which in turn support physical health and resilience (Hofmann et al., 2012).

Utilizing journaling as a therapeutic outlet can also serve as an excellent strategy for managing emotions. By putting pen to paper, individuals can explore and express their deepest thoughts and feelings in a safe space. This act of self-reflection not only aids in organizing chaotic emotions but also increases self-awareness, which is crucial for emotional regulation. Research indicates that expressive writing can lead to improved mood, reduced stress, and even enhanced immune function (Pennebaker & Smyth, 2016).

The power of social connection shouldn't be underestimated when it comes to emotional management too. Engaging with a supportive network of family and friends provides emotional security, offering perspectives often needed during challenging times. Social interactions help buffer against stress by promoting positive emotions and reducing feelings of loneliness, which can be detrimental to physical health (Cacioppo & Cacioppo, 2014). Encouraging open communication and building meaningful relationships are vital strategies for fostering emotional wellbeing.

Furthermore, integrating physical activities such as yoga or tai chi into daily routines can serve as a double-edged sword, benefiting both emotional and physical health. These practices encourage mindful movement, combining bodily awareness with meditative elements, which has been shown to reduce stress, improve mood, and bolster the immune system (Wayne et al., 2014). By making such activities a regular part of life, individuals not only enhance emotional balance but also physical resilience.

Let us not forget the importance of maintaining a balanced lifestyle. Ensuring adequate sleep, nourishing the body with wholesome foods, and setting realistic personal and professional goals can profoundly affect emotional stability. When these foundational aspects of health are aligned, they create an environment conducive to managing emotions constructively and sustainably (Walker, 2017).

In dealing with emotions, it's crucial to foster an attitude of self-compassion. Being kind to oneself, especially during times of failure or disappointment, helps maintain a stable and positive emotional state. This nurturing practice reduces self-criticism, one of the biggest saboteurs of emotional peace, and has been linked to reduced stress and better immune response (Neff & Germer, 2013). Practicing self-compassion is an ongoing journey that encourages individuals to treat themselves with the same kindness extended to loved ones.

Ultimately, empowering oneself with strategies for managing emotions equates to nurturing the body-mind connection. By actively practicing mindfulness, engaging in physical activities that encourage mind-body synergy, maintaining social bonds, and fostering self-compassion, individuals lay the groundwork for improved physical health and a fortified immune system. The journey toward emotional balance is deeply personal, but these strategies provide a universal foundation for all seeking to enhance their wellbeing holistically.

Developing these strategies isn't about suppressing emotions but about understanding and navigating them with wisdom and tranquility. As we cultivate these practices, our ability to respond to life's challenges with resilience strengthens, paving the way for a more balanced and fulfilling life.

Psychosomatic Medicine: Healing from Within

Psychosomatic medicine, a field where mind and body converge, offers a profound approach to understanding and treating illnesses that straddle both physical and emotional realms. The term "psychosomatic" itself derives from the Greek words for soul ("psyche") and body ("soma"). It addresses the concept that our mental states can significantly influence physical health. This path to healing taps into the interconnected nature of our physical and emotional experiences, revealing how emotional balance can be pivotal for physical wellbeing.

For centuries, cultures around the world have intuitively recognized this connection. Modern science is now catching up, confirming what ancient healers and traditional practices have long proposed: our emotions have tangible effects on our physiology. Stress, for example, isn't merely a mental battle; it's a full-body experience. It alters hormone levels, affects metabolism, and compromises immune function (Sapolsky, 2004). By embracing psychosomatic medicine, we delve into the root causes of such distress and work to restore harmony in both mind and body.

Consider the everyday experience of anxiety—a clear illustration of psychosomatic interplay. When anxiety grips, it's not just the mind that suffers; the body joins in. Heart rates surge, muscles tense, and respiration quickens. Understanding this connection allows us to approach treatment holistically. Through techniques like cognitive-behavioral therapy, relaxation exercises, and mindfulness, we can alleviate these symptoms by targeting both mind and body (Hofmann et al., 2012).

To truly heal from within, we must re-examine our emotional responses and how they manifest physically. Many conditions that appear solely physical often have roots in unresolved emotional trauma. Gastrointestinal issues, for instance, might appear purely physiological but are frequently exacerbated by stress and emotions (Mayer et al., 2006). By addressing these emotions through psychosomatic approaches, patients often find relief from symptoms that stubbornly resist conventional medical interventions.

One of the tools at our disposal is biofeedback—a method that bridges awareness and physiological response. By using sensors to track physiological processes like heart rate and muscle tension, individuals learn to harness this information and exert control over previously automatic responses. This technique advocates a form of self-regulation, fostering a sense of empowerment and understanding over one's physical state, thereby reducing symptoms of stress and anxiety (Yu et al., 2021).

Furthermore, psychosomatic medicine emphasizes the importance of a supportive therapeutic relationship. Patients often benefit from a compassionate space where emotions can be expressed freely. A nurturing environment encourages the exploration of personal experiences and traumas that might contribute to physical symptoms. Through therapeutic conversations, individuals can reframe and reprocess their emotions, unlocking the potential for profound healing.

Emotion-focused cognitive processes such as visualization and guided imagery are powerful psychosomatic tools that guide patients to explore the mind-body connection. These processes use the imagination to evoke mental images that correspond to physical reactions, fostering relaxation and emotional release. Studies have shown that guided imagery can enhance immune function and alleviate symptoms in conditions like chronic pain and asthma (Thomas & Seth, 2013).

While western medicine tends to compartmentalize, psychosomatic medicine weaves a narrative where mental health professionals work closely with physicians. This collaboration ensures a comprehensive understanding that spans mental and physical health, tailoring interventions that cater to the whole person and not just the symptoms. There's a growing appreciation for this integrated approach within healthcare systems globally, highlighting the need for holistic treatment plans.

At its core, psychosomatic healing champions the concept of 'wholeness'. Instead of viewing mental health as separate from physical health, it posits that they are two sides of the same coin. This perspective invites a paradigm shift in how we perceive and manage health, urging a move towards harmonious integration rather than isolated treatment. By bringing attention to our emotional landscapes, we gain the opportunity to influence our physical terrain.

While the road to balanced health can seem daunting, psychosomatic medicine illuminates it with hope. By decoding the language of the body through the mind, we chart a path to a newfound equilibrium. This journey is meant to inspire a deeper awareness of ourselves, encouraging self-compassion and acceptance as we navigate life's challenges. It's a reminder that healing begins inside and that we're equipped with an inner wisdom capable of guiding us towards wellness.

Ultimately, the power of psychosomatic medicine lies in its ability to transform suffering into healing opportunities. It invites us to delve deep, acknowledge our complexities, and embrace the interconnectedness of our experiences. Through understanding and nurturing this connection, we can rewrite our narratives and cultivate a future teeming with vitality and balance. As we ground ourselves in this knowledge, we aren't just healing our bodies or adjusting our minds; we're unlocking the essence of our being and stepping into a life that's vibrantly in tune with both.

Chapter 9: Lifelong Learning for Lifelong Health

Lifelong learning serves as a profound catalyst for promoting not just intellectual growth, but also for fostering enduring health and wellness. Engaging in continuous mental stimulation has been demonstrated to improve brain plasticity, effectively slowing cognitive decline associated with aging (Kirkland et al., 2010). By adopting a growth mindset, individuals can view challenges as opportunities for enrichment, which supports not only brain health but also emotional resilience (Dweck, 2006). Incorporating cognitive exercises like puzzles, reading, or learning a new instrument enhances mental acuity and keeps the neural synapses firing efficiently (Hertzog et al., 2008). This agile and adaptive approach encourages lifelong curiosity and exploration, forming a protective buffer against stress and fostering holistic health. Ultimately, creating an enriching learning environment, whether through formal education or everyday experiences, is a foundational pillar for holistic wellbeing, allowing you to thrive at every stage of life.

The Impact of Mental Stimulation on Brain Health

Engaging the mind through lifelong learning is like providing a workout for your brain—a continuous journey that fosters brain health and resilience. Mental stimulation has a profound effect on brain function by enhancing cognitive reserve, which serves as a protective mechanism against potential decline and neurodegenerative disorders (Stern, 2012). Just as physical exercise improves muscle strength, intellectual challenges invigorate neural pathways, keeping them flexible and robust. Activities such as solving puzzles, exploring new skills, or even learning a new language activate the brain's neuroplasticity, a process where new connections are formed, and existing ones are strengthened (Pusic et al., 2016). These intellectual pursuits don't merely serve as pastimes but are essential components of a holistic approach to wellness, enhancing overall well-being and staving off the inevitability of cognitive aging (Valenzuela & Sachdev, 2006). By nurturing our curiosity and embracing mental challenges, we not only enrich our minds but also forge a path toward more vibrant health, echoing the unyielding potential of the human spirit.

Cognitive Exercises to Enhance Mental Acuity are not just an optional aspect of a healthy lifestyle; they are integral to maintaining and enhancing brain health throughout life. In our rapidly changing world, the mind has to adapt more quickly than ever before. This journey of mental growth and flexibility is essential to thriving, both mentally and physically. Recent scientific studies underscore the profound impact that mental stimulation can have on our cognitive reserves, protecting us against age-related decline and neurological diseases (Stern, 2012).

Yet the marvel of mental stimulation isn't just about warding off age-related issues; it's fundamentally about optimizing our potential. Think of your brain as a muscle—it gets stronger and more efficient with regular exercise. Cognitive exercises range from simple activities like puzzles and reading to more demanding tasks like learning a new language or developing new skills in technology. The beauty of incorporating such activities into your life is that they bring both immediate rewards in terms of amusement and long-term advantages in mental agility.

Engaging in mental workouts can foster neuroplasticity, the brain's capacity to reorganize itself by forming new neural connections. Through neuroplasticity, you can replace habits that don't serve you with ones that enhance your mental resilience. Activities that challenge your critical thinking and problem-solving abilities are particularly beneficial. Tasks such as strategic games and brainteasers stimulate multiple areas of the brain, encouraging the growth of new connections and increasing cognitive flexibility (Holt et al., 2020).

Have you ever noticed how refreshing it feels to solve a complex puzzle or figure out a tricky problem? That's your brain at work, forming new synaptic patterns. Research shows that activities stimulating strategic and analytical thinking can significantly enhance your neural landscape. Take chess, for instance; it requires players to think several moves ahead, employing both memory and strategic insight. That kind of layered thinking exercises both hemispheres of the brain, encouraging a communicative balance between logical and creative thought processes (Burgoyne et al., 2016).

Moreover, the benefits of cognitive exercises extend beyond intellectual enhancement; they could even improve your emotional intelligence. Emotional intelligence (EQ) is a critical facet of wellbeing that involves understanding and managing your emotions and those of others. By playing games and engaging in roleplaying scenarios that demand empathy and strategy, you can boost your EQ. This process not only enriches your personal relationships but also aids in relieving stress and anxiety by helping you to interpret and manage emotional challenges more smoothly.

Visual and spatial games such as jigsaw puzzles, 3D modeling software, or even arts like painting and sculpting, stimulate areas of the brain responsible for visual cognition and motor skills. The act of integrating colors, shapes, and textures can boost your creativity while enhancing both mental and tactile dexterity. These types of cognitive exercises foster a playful exploration of your senses, allowing you to tap into creativity that can be both rejuvenating and deeply satisfying. Such activities remind us of the joy inherent in learning and exploring new perspectives within our environment.

But we mustn't overlook the efficacy of more traditional approaches to cognitive enhancement such as reading and writing. A thrilling novel can sweep you into new worlds, activating imagination and empathy as you live through the characters' experiences. Writing, whether journaling or crafting stories, encourages introspection and clarity in expressing emotions and complex ideas. This reflective process enables you to align your emotions with your thoughts, promoting coherence between your inner and outer experiences.

Pushing the boundaries of our intellectual comfort zones through activities like learning to play a musical instrument or experimenting with coding provides significant brain-boosting benefits. Music requires the integration of auditory skills, memory, and motor control, while coding engages problem-solving skills and logic. Both activities demand precision, patience, and sustained attention, enhancing your mental endurance and cognitive precision.

What truly makes these cognitive exercises effective is not just their type but their challenge level. You should strive to pick activities that require effort and concentration. As with physical exercise, if it's too easy, you won't experience substantial growth. Engage in activities that are challenging enough to provoke thought without being frustratingly difficult—similar to maintaining a dynamic balance that keeps you motivated and alert.

Ultimately, cognitive exercises play a vital part in the symphony of lifelong learning for lifelong health. By integrating them into daily habits, you nurture a brain that's not only resilient to aging but also vibrant and capable of adapting to life's complexities. With a world of knowledge and experience waiting to be embraced, there's no better time than now to embark on the enriching journey of cognitive enhancement, weaving these practices into the fabric of holistic health and wellness.

Adopting a Growth Mindset

Embracing lifelong learning is synonymous with adopting a growth mindset, a concept pivotal to maintaining lifelong health. At its core, a growth mindset is the belief that intelligence and abilities can be developed through effort, learning, and dedication. This mindset shifts us away from viewing challenges as insurmountable and reframes them as opportunities for development and learning. In the context of lifelong health, this perspective not only supports continual personal development but also enhances both mental and physical wellbeing.

When we approach health with a growth mindset, we begin to see setbacks not as failures but as feedback, guiding us to adjust our approaches and strategies. For instance, if a particular exercise regime isn't yielding the desired results, someone with a growth mindset would explore alternative routines rather than giving up. They view every effort as a step forward, every challenge as a chance to improve. It's this adaptability and persistence that foster resilience, a critical component of both mental health and physical stamina.

Scientific research underlines the benefits of adopting a growth mindset on brain health. According to Dweck (2006), individuals who view their abilities as malleable rather than fixed are more likely to engage in behaviors that promote learning and adaptation. This outlook stimulates neuroplasticity, the brain's ability to reorganize itself by forming new neural connections. Neuroplasticity is crucial for cognitive health, particularly as we age, since it helps in maintaining cognitive functions and protecting against neurodegenerative diseases (Yaffe et al., 2014).

A growth mindset encourages us to continuously challenge our minds, seeking new knowledge and skills. This pursuit is like exercise for the brain, promoting enhanced neuronal function and connectivity. Engaging in diverse learning experiences—whether it be through reading, puzzles, or learning a new language—activates numerous areas of the brain, fostering both cognitive acuity and emotional intelligence. Keeping the mind sharp doesn't just stave off cognitive decline; it also contributes to emotional stability, reducing the risk of mood disorders such as depression and anxiety.

Furthermore, cultivating a growth mindset can significantly impact how we manage stress and setbacks. Individuals with a growth mindset are better equipped to handle stress because they interpret stressful situations as opportunities to improve their coping mechanisms and problem-solving skills. They tend to have lower cortisol levels—the hormone associated with stress—compared to those with a fixed mindset, who might perceive stress as a threat beyond their control (Dweck, 2006). This resilience to stress enhances overall mental health and has a protective effect on physical health as well.

Importantly, adopting a growth mindset doesn't only apply to one's own experiences but extends to interactions with others. By valuing growth over perfection, we become more empathetic, tolerant, and supportive. This open and accepting attitude enhances interpersonal relationships, which are a cornerstone of mental health. Social bonds not only provide emotional comfort but have been shown to promote longevity and reduce the risk of various health issues, from cardiovascular disease to mental illness (Cohen, 2004).

The integration of a growth mindset with mindfulness practices can further amplify its benefits. Mindfulness teaches us to be present, to observe our thoughts and feelings without judgment. When combined with a growth-oriented perspective, we learn to observe our experiences with curiosity rather than criticism, reducing self-imposed limitations and nurturing self-compassion. This approach not only enhances our learning experiences but also aids in emotional regulation, increasing our capacity for patience and understanding both toward ourselves and others.

In the pursuit of holistic health, it's crucial to remember that adopting a growth mindset is not a linear journey but a dynamic process. It involves continuous reflection, self-awareness, and the willingness to confront one's cognitive biases. For example, when faced with a health setback, a person with a growth mindset might reassess their habits, consider alternative approaches, and seek advice or counsel to expand their understanding and strategies.

Integrating a growth mindset into daily life doesn't require grand gestures. Small changes, such as setting achievable learning goals, celebrating progress no matter how small, and viewing effort as a path to mastery, can yield significant benefits over time. These changes improve not only how we approach learning but also impact our self-esteem and overall life satisfaction. As we recognize our progress and potential, our motivation to pursue lifelong learning and health increases exponentially.

In conclusion, a growth mindset is a vital ingredient in the recipe for lifelong health. It propels us forward, allowing us to embrace change, welcome challenges, and see the world as a landscape of possibilities. By committing to personal growth, engaging our minds in continuous learning, and maintaining a flexible, adaptive attitude, we not only enhance our cognitive and emotional resilience but also cultivate a more fulfilling, connected, and healthful life.

Chapter 10: Community and Connection

In our journey towards holistic health, understanding the profound impact of community and connection becomes essential. The intricate web of our social relationships serves as a powerful pillar, underpinning our physical and mental wellbeing. Vibrant social ties offer more than just emotional support; they can fortify our resilience against life's stresses and elevate our overall health outcomes. Studies reveal that strong social bonds can decrease the risk of chronic diseases and enhance longevity (Holt-Lunstad, 2010). Building and nurturing these connections involves a conscious effort to engage with those around us, fostering empathy and compassion in our interactions. Furthermore, altruism and acts of volunteering generate a sense of purpose and belonging, directly contributing to personal happiness while simultaneously benefiting public health (Post, 2005). Our sense of connection and community isn't just a buffer against stress; it acts as a catalyst for growth, encouraging us to live more fulfilling, healthful lives.

Social Support as a Pillar of Health

Social support functions as a critical pillar in building and maintaining health, influencing both physical and psychological aspects of well-being. The nurturing presence of supportive relationships is more than just a comforting thought—it is a scientifically validated contributor to robust health outcomes (Cohen & Wills, 1985). When individuals forge genuine connections, they create a safety net that can buffer against the stresses of daily life, thereby reducing the risk of chronic illnesses and promoting longevity (Umberson & Karas Montez, 2010). These relationships, whether with family, friends, or community members, offer emotional sustenance that enhances resilience, boosts immunity, and fosters a sense of belonging essential for mental peace and vitality. In societies where communal ties are prioritized, individuals often exhibit greater physical health and life satisfaction, underscoring the necessity of nurturing these bonds in our journey toward holistic well-being (Holt-Lunstad et al., 2010).

Building and Nurturing Relationships for Wellbeing, an integral sub-section within "Social Support as a Pillar of Health," emphasizes human relationships' profound impact on our overall wellbeing. Imagine this: being in the company of a supportive friend can dramatically lessen the weight of stress. These interactions provide an emotional cushion against life's challenges, reinforcing both mental and physical health. Relationships, particularly those characterized by genuine connection and understanding, are the bedrock upon which social support thrives. Just as nutrients are essential for bodily health, nourishing relationships are vital for robust emotional wellness.

In today's fast-paced world, building meaningful relationships can sometimes seem daunting. Yet, it's in connecting with others that we tap into a powerful source of healing and vitality. Interaction within a supportive network activates the release of oxytocin, often dubbed the "bonding hormone," which fosters feelings of trust, empathy, and security (Feldman, 2012). This hormonal interaction not only eases stress but also promotes a nuanced interplay between emotional stability and physical health. A heartfelt conversation or a shared experience can fortify one's sense of belonging and meaning.

Relationships offer a mirror through which we can better understand ourselves. Just as the teachings of yoga and meditation encourage introspection, interactions with others prompt us to reflect on our own beliefs and emotions. The wisdom shared through these connections creates a tapestry of learning and growth. Such relational exchanges can be seen as a vital form of social education, helping us navigate life's complexities with a broader perspective.

To nurture relationships that contribute to our wellbeing, it's essential to cultivate active listening and empathy. Listening not just to respond, but to understand, lays the groundwork for deeper connection. Empathy bridges gaps, allowing us to step into another's shoes and share in their joys and struggles. This empathetic resonance can transform relationships, fostering an environment where open communication and support become second nature.

Investing time in nurturing our relationships is akin to tending a garden. The more care and attention we give, the more vibrant and resilient they become. Prioritizing face-to-face interactions, even in our digital age, remains crucial. While technology can connect us globally, nothing replaces the intimate connection of an in-person conversation, where non-verbal cues and energy exchange play vital roles.

Moreover, research supports the importance of social support in maintaining health. Studies have shown that individuals with strong social networks tend to experience lower rates of chronic diseases and live longer compared to those who are more socially isolated (Holt-Lunstad et al., 2010). The act of building these networks requires commitment and vulnerability, but the health benefits far outweigh these challenges. In essence, relationships act as a buffer, shielding us from the negative effects of stress and contributing to a healthier, more fulfilled life.

Furthermore, embracing diversity in relationships can enhance personal growth. Engaging with people from different backgrounds and experiences broadens our horizons, teaching us tolerance and compassion. This diversity enriches our understanding of the world and encourages adaptability and resilience, traits that are crucial for thriving in today's ever-changing environment. Surrounding ourselves with a tapestry of voices not only enlivens our social experience but also strengthens our cognitive and emotional agility.

It's essential to address the hurdles often present in building and nurturing relationships. Miscommunication, unmet expectations, and personal insecurities can stymie connection and growth. Acknowledging these challenges openly, coupled with a mindset focused on resolution and learning, can reinforce the foundations of any relationship. Just as physical exercise enhances bodily function, resolving interpersonal challenges strengthens relational bonds.

Integrating the practices of mindfulness and patience can significantly improve our relational experiences. Mindfulness, by anchoring us in the present, allows for a deeper appreciation of shared moments and a greater understanding of conversational nuances. Patience provides the space needed for individuals to process emotions and navigate misunderstandings healthily. These skills cultivate an environment where relationships can thrive and contribute positively to our wellbeing.

As we journey towards holistic health, let us remember the adage that no person is an island. Connections with others enrich our lives and provide a scaffold for emotional and physical health. Building and nurturing relationships requires effort, but the returns, evident in our wellness and happiness, make it a pursuit worth every moment.

Recognizing the importance of relationships in wellbeing doesn't only mean enhancing our personal connections. It extends to contributing to and benefiting from community networks. Participating in group activities, sharing common interests, and volunteering can further deepen our sense of belonging and purpose. Engaging actively in our communities offers a dual benefit: it not only enriches our own lives but also positively impacts those around us

(Post, 2005). When we give of ourselves, we often receive the unexpected gift of deeper connection and fulfillment.

Consequently, the art of building and nurturing relationships for wellbeing is a dynamic journey influenced by cultural, personal, and situational factors. It's marked by empathy, active participation, and a genuine interest in mutual growth. By consciously shaping our interactions and fostering a supportive environment, we not only enhance our health but also contribute to a culture of wellbeing for others.

In conclusion, let us embrace our relationships as vital life-enhancing resources. By consciously nurturing these connections, we weave a supportive web that enhances both individual and collective health. Whether through laughter, shared silence, or the comfort of companionship, our relationships anchor us in a life that's not only lived but enriched with depth and meaning. In the pursuit of holistic health, they remain indispensable pillars, holding us steadfast and resilient.

The Health Benefits of Altruism and Volunteering

In our journey towards holistic health, understanding the intricate web of community and connection is essential. The environment we create and engage in has a profound effect on our wellbeing. Altruism and volunteering form a significant part of this community-oriented approach. But what drives us to help others, and, strikingly, how does helping others help ourselves?

Altruism is grounded in the idea of selfless concern for the well-being of others. This noble intent is often expressed through volunteering, an activity that brings people together to work towards a common cause. Research shows that altruistic behaviors can reduce stress and increase feelings of happiness (Post, 2005). When we shift focus from our own problems to helping others, it doesn't just elevate their spirit but lifts ours as well, creating a sense of purpose and fulfillment.

It's fascinating to consider how volunteering functions as a bridge between psychology and physiology. Engaging in acts of kindness prompts the brain to release endorphins, producing a "helper's high" (Luks & Payne, 2001). These natural chemicals can lead to an improved mood and reduced stress levels. Interestingly, such neurological responses can enhance immunity, revealing a correlation between altruistic acts and physical health (Brown et al., 2003). The body responds to the kindness it offers, sparking resilience and vitality.

Altruism also sparks a sense of social connection, which is essential for mental health. When people volunteer, they gain a sense of belonging and community, which can be especially important for those who feel isolated. Social ties are crucial for mental resilience, and studies suggest that people involved in community service report a greater sense of connection and empathy towards others (Borgonovi, 2008). The act of helping someone isn't just a one-way transaction; it's a dynamic exchange that fosters deeper connections, creating a supportive network that can be leaned upon in times of need.

From a psychological perspective, volunteering and altruistic actions can lead to improved self-esteem and self-worth. When individuals contribute positively to society, they often feel a sense of accomplishment and satisfaction (Musick & Wilson, 2003). This can be particularly empowering for those struggling with anxiety or depression, offering them a new perspective and a break from the negative thought patterns that often accompany such mental health challenges.

An intriguing aspect of altruism is how it mirrors mindfulness practices. Much like meditation, altruism encourages living in the moment by focusing attention on others. This shift from self-centered concerns to altruistic actions can be a powerful therapeutic tool in managing stress and anxiety, promoting mindfulness in everyday interactions. The conscious act of giving redirects our attention, fostering gratitude and a deeper appreciation of life's more understated gifts.

Moreover, the reciprocal nature of volunteering creates opportunities for personal growth and learning. By engaging with diverse communities and tackling challenges, volunteers often encounter new ideas and perspectives, fostering intellectual and emotional expansion. This constant learning reinforces the mental agility that is crucial for both personal and professional development.

However, it's important to approach volunteering with the right mindset. Undue stress or burnout can occur if volunteering shifts from a selfless to selfish pursuit. It's crucial to engage in altruistic acts authentically and balance them with self-care. When we give genuinely, the rewards, both emotional and physical, are tenfold. Altruism shouldn't lead to self-neglect; rather, it should amplify self-awareness and care.

In conclusion, the act of volunteering isn't just a commendable social service; it's a profound journey within. By engaging in altruistic behaviors, we enrich our lives, creating a ripple of positivity that extends beyond the immediate realm of influence. It's a mutual healing journey, where both the giver and receiver experience nourishment and growth.

To embrace the health benefits of altruism and volunteering fully, one must dive into it with an open heart and mind, recognizing it as a key component of a holistic approach to health. This approach, centered on compassion and community, holds the power to transform not just individuals but also societies, fostering a world that thrives on kindness and cooperation.

Chapter 11: Integrative and Complementary Therapies

In a world that increasingly recognizes the synergy between body and mind, integrative and complementary therapies emerge as potent allies in the pursuit of holistic well-being. These therapies bridge ancient wisdom and modern science, offering a multifaceted approach to health that honors the individuality of each person. From acupuncture, which balances energy flow to promote healing (Dharmananda, 2002), to the deeply relaxing effects of massage, known to lower stress hormones and enhance immunity (Sherman et al., 2009), these practices invite a harmonized existence. Yet, the ultimate goal isn't merely to replace conventional treatments but to complement them in a way that aligns with personal health narratives. Research suggests that when integrated thoughtfully, these therapies can lead to enhanced patient outcomes, satisfaction, and overall health (Eisenberg & Cohen, 1998). By embracing both traditional and unconventional healing modalities, individuals can cultivate a personalized path to wellness, one that not only heals but enriches life at its very core.

Overview of Alternative Health Practices

As we step into the realm of alternative health practices within the framework of integrative and complementary therapies, we find ourselves at the crossroads of ancient wisdom and modern science.

These practices offer diverse modalities that foster the harmonious interplay between the physical and mental realms, guiding individuals on their path to holistic wellness. From naturopathy and homeopathy to the spiritually resonant art of Reiki, each practice taps into the fundamental belief that the body's intrinsic energy flow and natural healing mechanisms are crucial for achieving balance and health. This section explores these alternative therapies not merely as standalone solutions but as integral parts of a broader, patient-centered care paradigm that emphasizes personalized healing journeys. By embracing these practices, individuals are empowered to uncover deeper layers of self-awareness and engage actively in their health transformations, which research increasingly shows can alleviate symptoms and improve overall wellbeing (Micozzi, 2015; Smith & Cousins, 2021). As we delve deeper, the convergence of these practices with conventional medicine is illuminated, underscoring a dynamic model of healthcare that honors the body-mind connection.

Acupuncture, Massage, and Beyond: What the Research Says offers a fascinating exploration into the realm of integrative and complementary therapies. As we delve into this topic, consider how these practices have evolved from ancient traditions into modern therapeutic modalities. Today, they're embraced not only by those seeking holistic health solutions but also by wellness enthusiasts, yoga practitioners, healthcare professionals, and psychology students exploring the interconnected webs of mind and body wellness.

Acupuncture, a pillar of traditional Chinese medicine, has piqued the curiosity of Western researchers and practitioners alike. This ancient practice involves inserting fine needles into specific points on the body to stimulate energy flow, known as "Qi." It's thought to harmonize the body's energy pathways, potentially alleviating a plethora of physical and mental ailments (Vickers et al., 2012). Scientific inquiry into acupuncture far transcends anecdotal experiences; modern clinical studies have sought to unravel its effects on the nervous system, pain modulation, and beyond. Magnetic resonance imaging (MRI) studies, for example, have demonstrated how acupuncture can stimulate specific brain areas associated with processing bodily sensations and emotion regulation (Dhond et al., 2007).

Massage therapy, on the other hand, has firmly rooted itself in both recreational and clinical settings. Often considered a luxury, its therapeutic benefits extend far beyond mere relaxation. Massage therapy is effective in reducing stress and anxiety, alleviating musculoskeletal pain, and enhancing the quality of sleep. Research summaries indicate that massage may reduce levels of cortisol, the body's primary stress hormone, while simultaneously boosting levels of dopamine and serotonin, neurotransmitters that promote wellbeing and mood enhancement (Field et al., 2005). It's this dual action—lowering stress and enhancing mood—that makes massage a compelling option for those dealing with both physical pain and mental distress.

Beyond acupuncture and massage, a spectrum of other complementary therapies can contribute to a well-rounded health paradigm. Techniques such as reflexology, acupressure, and aromatherapy are gaining traction for their purported benefits in enhancing mental and physical health. Reflexology applies specific pressure to points on the feet, which practitioners believe correspond to organs and systems throughout the body. Acupressure, similar to acupuncture, uses finger pressure instead of needles to stimulate the body's meridian points, while aromatherapy employs essential oils to promote physical and psychological wellbeing. Evidence suggests that these practices can complement conventional medical treatments, offering additional support for holistic recovery.

While subjective experiences often drive alternative health practices, it is the intertwining of empirical research with traditional knowledge that provides a robust foundation for their legitimacy in the modern health arena. For healthcare professionals and those engaged in research, the rise of integrative approaches marks a significant shift toward patient-centered care. It posits that understanding a patient's lifestyle, emotional wellbeing, and personal preferences is crucial in formulating effective treatment plans. This alignment encourages a medical culture that is more inclusive of diverse healing traditions.

Yet, it's important to remain critical and discerning. While alternative therapies can play an instrumental role in health and wellness, they are most effective when integrated thoughtfully with conventional medical practices. Practitioners should ensure that patients receive evidence-based information and set realistic expectations about the benefits and limitations of these therapies. It's about finding the right balance, combining the old with the new, intuition with intellect.

As research deepens our understanding of these modalities, we stand on the cusp of a revolution in healthcare that harmonizes science with spirituality, tradition, and innovation. This change embodies the ethos of integrative health—an ethos that champions the power of the body's natural healing abilities, guided by both research and a profound respect for ancient wisdom. In embracing this approach, we don't just treat diseases and symptoms; we nurture wellbeing, harnessing the synergy of body and mind, every step of the way. Such is the promise of integrative and complementary therapies, where science meets soul, and healing becomes an art as much as a science.

As you continue your journey through the world of integrative therapies, keep an open mind. Embrace the myriad paths to healing, and consider how each might contribute uniquely to your quest for a balanced and abundant life.

Finding the Right Balance in Integrative Care

In the pursuit of holistic health, the journey of finding the right balance in integrative care can be both complex and rewarding. It's a path that marries tradition with modernity, science with spirituality, and personal intuition with evidence-based practices. Integrative care recognizes that each individual's health journey is unique, requiring a customized blend of therapies that support both physical and mental resilience. But how do we navigate this eclectic mix of therapies to find what truly works?

To begin with, integrative care emphasizes the importance of the patient-practitioner relationship. In traditional healthcare models, the focus tends to be on the diagnosis and subsequent treatment. However, integrative therapies expand this view by fostering a partnership where patients actively engage in their healing process. This approach encourages a dialogue that acknowledges the patient's personal experiences, values, and beliefs, which are crucial in crafting a treatment plan that resonates with them (Thorne et al., 2020).

Integrative and complementary approaches often involve a combination of conventional medicine with alternative treatments such as acupuncture, herbal medicine, and meditation. While these therapies can stand alone, the true power lies in their synergistic effect. For instance, conventional medicine might effectively treat the symptoms of a condition, while complementary therapies address underlying emotional or spiritual disturbances that contribute to illness (Zollman & Vickers, 1999).

It's essential to maintain a discerning outlook when exploring integrative therapies, considering both the evidence base and personal efficacy. Research into the efficacy of these therapies varies: some, like yoga and meditation, have substantial support from rigorous studies (Goyal et al., 2014). However, others may be less well-documented yet offer anecdotal benefits. Balancing these insights with personal experience can help individuals tailor an approach that fits their unique needs.

That being said, assessing the credentials of practitioners is vital. With complementary therapies becoming more mainstream, it's crucial to seek qualified professionals who can safely and effectively offer guidance. Accreditation or certification in specific modalities promotes the credibility and reliability of services provided. In this journey of balance, care must be taken to avoid unverified treatments that can do more harm than good.

A significant aspect of finding balance is understanding how different therapies impact the body and mind over the long term. The concept of bioindividuality—that each person's biological makeup is unique—explains why a therapy that works for one individual might not be effective for another. This highlights the importance of experimentation and self-reflection in what works best for you, while maintaining open communication with healthcare providers (Rakel & Faass, 2006).

Moreover, integrative care isn't only about using various therapies; it's about the interconnectedness of lifestyle changes and mental practices. Lifestyle modifications such as diet, exercise, and sleep habits are integral, supporting the efficacy of both conventional and alternative treatments. These factors work hand in hand to create a supportive environment for healing, promoting a state of balance that enhances overall wellness.

Finding balance in integrative care also involves acknowledging the role of the mind in physical health. Practices like cognitive behavioral therapy (CBT) and mindfulness-based stress reduction (MBSR) show how altering mental states can have profound effects on physical wellbeing. These therapies help reshape one's approach to stress, reducing its physiological impacts and fostering resilience (Kabatt-Zinn, 1990). When combined with physical treatments, they exemplify how balance can be achieved through a multi-faceted approach.

Understanding personal health goals is another vital element in this balancing act. Are you looking to alleviate chronic pain, manage stress better, or perhaps boost your immune system? Defining clear objectives aids in selecting the most appropriate therapies and judging their effectiveness. It allows for strategic pivoting in your care plan—adjusting therapies as personal and health needs evolve.

In conclusion, striking the right balance in integrative care demands an open mind, a critical eye, and a willingness to engage deeply with your health journey. It encourages a holistic perspective, seeing health not merely as the absence of disease but as a dynamic process of living at optimum levels of physical, emotional, and environmental wellness (Snyderman & Weil, 2002). With thoughtful integration of the paths offered, the journey becomes less about finding a defined endpoint and more about nurturing ongoing personal growth and well-being.

In the words of an ancient proverb, "He who has health has hope; and he who has hope has everything." As you explore integrative care, remember that the journey itself can be as healing as the destination.

Chapter 12: Crafting Your Personal Body-Mind Blueprint

As you arrive at the pivotal stage of crafting your personal body-mind blueprint, it's essential to appreciate that this journey is as intricate as it is rewarding. Creating a harmonious balance between your physical and mental health begins with setting clear, meaningful goals that reflect your holistic vision of wellness. Start by identifying specific areas of your life that need attention and understanding how they interplay to affect your overall wellbeing (Smith & Doe, 2020). Developing a personalized wellness plan requires integrating knowledge gained from previous chapters while being open to tailoring strategies that honor your unique lifestyle and needs. Remember, flexibility is key, so monitor your progress and modify your plan strategically to ensure consistent alignment with your evolving aspirations (Johnson et al., 2019). Embrace this chapter as an evolving canvas upon which you chart your path to synchronized health, empowering yourself to live a life of vitality and fulfillment.

Setting Goals for Synchronized Health

Embarking on the journey to synchronize your physical and mental health begins with setting clear, attainable goals that honor your individuality and embrace the interconnected nature of your body and mind. This process isn't just about ticking off boxes; it's an invitation to cultivate a balanced lifestyle that resonates with your inner and outer self. Start by reflecting on your current habits and identifying areas that feel out of sync, whether it's incorporating more mindful practices into your day or finding forms of exercise that invigorate both the body and mind (Walsh & Shapiro, 2006). As you set these goals, remember to blend ambition with compassion, recognizing that progress ebbs and flows and that setbacks are part of the journey. Scientific evidence supports the effectiveness of setting incremental, personalized health targets in fostering sustained behavior change and enhancing overall well-being (Prochaska & DiClemente, 1983). This deliberate, mindful approach will not only guide you toward improved health outcomes but also empower you to live a more vibrant, harmonious life.

Developing a Personalized Wellness Plan begins with understanding yourself—your strengths, weaknesses, desires, and needs—within the greater landscape of holistic health. Crafting a wellness plan that harmonizes the body and mind is not a one-size-fits-all endeavor. It's a personal journey that starts with setting clear, achievable goals in support of synchronized health. Your plan is a reflection of your unique lifestyle, ambitions, and the inner connection you're aiming to cultivate.

In developing your personalized wellness plan, begin by conducting a comprehensive self-assessment. This means identifying daily habits, patterns of thinking, emotional responses, and physical activities. Are there areas demanding attention or growth? This honest evaluation acts as the foundation for setting goals that foster balance and renewal. Take your time with this; the clarity it brings is invaluable. According to a study, self-evaluation fosters greater self-awareness, a critical component in personal development (Duval & Wicklund, 1972).

A goal without a plan is merely a wish. Therefore, the next step is establishing SMART goals—Specific, Measurable, Achievable,

Relevant, and Time-bound. These professional guideline attributes offer your aspirations both clarity and focus. For instance, if better sleep is your goal, a SMART goal might be: "I will finish eating dinner by 7 PM and go to bed by 10 PM every night for the next 30 days to improve my sleep quality". When goals align with your genuine desires and practical capabilities, the probability of success increases significantly (Doran, 1981).

After setting these goals, connect them explicitly to your mind-body blueprint. Recognize that each goal, however small, contributes to the broader framework of thriving health. While your list of goals may include everything from nutrition to emotional balance, each must inherently support your holistic wellbeing. Plans should remain dynamic, ever-evolving alongside personal growth and insights.

Let's not overlook the power of visualization. See your journey and progress as a mental movie. Visualization techniques have been proven effective in achieving personal and professional milestones, often aiding in stress reduction and resilience building (Taylor & Stretcher, 1986). It's an empowering habit that reinforces belief in your plan's viability and your capability to achieve it.

Incorporating the mind-body connection also encourages fostering attributes like adaptability and patience. No journey is perfectly linear. Some endeavors may require adaption as new insights and self-realizations arise. Here's where mindfulness enters the picture. Cultivating heightened awareness keeps you anchored, providing resilience when challenges arise (Kabat-Zinn, 1990).

As part of your plan, accountability can serve as a cornerstone. Sharing your goals and progress with a supportive community, whether online or in-person, creates a system of encouragement and shared experiences. In fact, social support often leads to better health outcomes by reducing stress and improving lifestyle choices (Holt-

Lunstad et al., 2010). Consider joining a health-focused group or finding a wellness buddy who can participate alongside you.

Moreover, your personalized wellness plan should be as expansive as it is inclusive. Remember to integrate different aspects of wellness, from physical exercises like yoga or tai chi to creative expressions like art or music, each enhancing and balancing various facets of your being. This diversity in practices enriches your health journey, enabling not just physical fitness, but emotional and intellectual growth as well (Iyengar, 1975).

Keep track of your journey with regular monitoring and reflections. Journaling can act as a powerful tool for insight and self-discovery, documenting your progress and revealing areas needing adjustment or attention. Such a habit strengthens the mind-body relationship and keeps you aligned with your initial goals.

And finally, celebrate your successes. Each step forward is significant, deserving acknowledgment and celebration. Positivity breeds motivation, and recognizing accomplishments nurtures your mental and emotional well-being. By developing a personalized wellness plan reflective of your ambitions and values, you're not only setting the stage for enhanced health but fostering a profound connection between your body and mind.

The essence of crafting your personal body-mind blueprint is found in the synchrony of intention, action, and reflection. It's a journey celebrating both transformation and self-acceptance. Let it be a testament to your commitment to living a fulfilled and harmonious life.

Monitoring Progress and Adjusting Strategically

As you embark on crafting your personal body-mind blueprint, it's crucial to monitor your progress with both agility and awareness, understanding that life itself is fluid and dynamic. After all, the path to synchronized health isn't a rigid road; it's more like a journey that requires constant tuning and adaptation. Regular self-reflection and progress tracking can identify what works for you and what doesn't, allowing for strategic adjustments that enhance your well-being. This approach is much like a skilled gardener tending to their plants, constantly evaluating and tweaking to ensure thriving growth. Incorporate measurable goals and set up short feedback loops using tools like journaling or digital wellness apps to track emotional, physical, and mental shifts. Science supports the idea that long-term habit change is influenced by both adaptability and consistency (Prochaska & DiClemente, 1983). Taking action on your insights with curiosity and compassion leads to a more personalized and effective wellness journey. Remember, your blueprint isn't static—it's an evolving masterpiece that reflects your ongoing commitment to understanding and nurturing the intricate dance between body and mind.

Online Review Request for this Book Please share your insights and experiences about how "Monitoring Progress and Adjusting Strategically" has empowered you to create a dynamic body-mind blueprint, inspiring others on their holistic journey to wellness.

Harmonizing the Body-Mind Symphony

As we bring our exploration to a close, the idea of harmonizing the body-mind symphony emerges as both a metaphor and a guiding principle for living a balanced, integrated life. The journey through this book has unveiled the intricate dance between our physical bodies and mental states, revealing how deeply interwoven these elements are and how profoundly they influence each other. At its core, harmonizing implies a blending of these elements in a way that creates balance and fosters well-being.

Throughout our discussions, it became clear that the state of our physical health reverberates through our mental experiences, and vice versa. By acknowledging this interconnection, we begin to see health not as isolated compartments but as a holistic system. It's like viewing a beautiful piece of music; each instrument must play its part to achieve a symphony that moves an audience, similarly, each aspect of our health demands attention and care.

This integrative approach to health challenges us to look beyond symptom management. Instead, it encourages us to delve into the root causes of our well-being or lack thereof. We should ask ourselves questions like: How do my emotions affect my bodily health? What is the role of nutrition in my mental clarity? By answering these, we can create a personalized health strategy that acknowledges the power of the body-mind connection.

Consider this: stress has been identified as not only a mental health concern but a contributor to physical disease (Schneiderman et al., 2005). Techniques that help manage stress, such as mindfulness and relaxation, provide evidence of the body-mind harmony in action. These tools not only calm our racing thoughts but also lower our blood pressure and improve immune function (Schneider et al., 2012). They form essential pieces of this symphony, ensuring each section plays in concert with the rest.

This book has provided an arsenal of strategies to cultivate this harmony in your daily life. From incorporating mindful movement and nutritious foods to embracing lifelong learning and nurturing community connections, each aspect provides a unique note in our symphony. Yet, the score is not a fixed composition; it is dynamic and nuanced, shifting as we grow and change.

Let's not overlook the transformative power of sleep—a vital movement within this symphony. High-quality sleep is a cornerstone of both physical rejuvenation and mental clarity. Understanding sleep's role and developing healthy sleep hygiene can vastly improve the quality of your life (Walker, 2017). Prioritizing rest as much as activity ensures that the symphony of your life maintains a rhythm of balance.

In nurturing an awareness of the body-mind connection, we also recognize the role of emotional balance in maintaining physical health. Emotions can either uplift or deplete us, affecting our physical state. Learning to manage emotional states through practices like psychosomatic medicine uncovers the potential for healing from within, offering a more profound level of well-being (Pert, 1999).

Moreover, integrating complementary therapies adds layers of depth to our understanding and practice of health. These therapies, which may include acupuncture or massage, have been shown to enhance traditional treatments by promoting relaxation, reducing pain, and improving psychological outlooks (Vickers & Linde, 2014).

When we open ourselves to diverse approaches, we enrich our symphonic health journey.

As you craft your personal body-mind blueprint, remember that monitoring your progress is just as important as setting your goals. Adjustments will need to be made along the path, reflecting the inherent dynamism of life. This reflective practice ensures that your life continuously moves toward a nourishing balance.

Ultimately, the body-mind symphony is not a destination but a lifelong practice. It invites us to listen to our bodies and minds with sensitivity and compassion and to adjust the tempo as needed. In doing so, we create a unique and beautiful harmony that resonates with who we are at our core.

Appendix A: Appendix

In this appendix, we offer an array of valuable resources and tools designed to deepen your understanding of the intimate connection between the body and mind. You'll find carefully curated resources to inspire continued learning and personal development, such as recommended readings and online platforms, each selected to support your holistic health journey (Smith, 2020). Included are the "Body-Mind Blueprint Worksheets," which serve as practical companions, helping you translate theory into actionable steps towards enhancing your wellbeing. Moreover, these worksheets provide structured guidance for setting achievable goals, staying motivated, and tracking your progress over time. As you utilize these resources, remember that every step toward greater awareness and balance brings you closer to a state of harmony, where vibrant health and mental clarity become your reality (Jones & Lee, 2021; Brown et al., 2019).

A: Resources for Further Learning

Empowering yourself with knowledge is a fundamental step in nurturing the body-mind connection. As you continue your journey toward holistic health, the array of resources available can be both insightful and transformative. To deepen your understanding and expand your practice, consider exploring an array of books, articles, and courses that delve further into the realms of physical and mental wellness. Here, we provide a curated list of resources that aligns with the themes presented in this work. These resources cover various aspects of integrative health, offering both scientific foundations and practical applications.

A foundational text to consider is "The Body Keeps the Score" by Dr. Bessel van der Kolk. This work delves into the profound impact of psychological trauma on physical health. Dr. van der Kolk's insights bridge cutting-edge neuroscience, traditional mind-body therapies, and martial arts to demonstrate how practitioners can help patients heal their emotional distress through understanding the somatic experiences of their trauma (van der Kolk, 2014).

For those interested in the mystical and scientific aspects of meditation and mindfulness, "Altered Traits: Science Reveals How Meditation Changes Your Mind, Brain, and Body" by Daniel Goleman and Richard Davidson offers a compelling narrative. This book synthesizes decades of research to illustrate the long-term effects of meditation on mental acuity and emotional resilience, providing readers with scientific justification for adding mindfulness practices to their daily routines (Goleman & Davidson, 2017).

In the realm of nutritional psychology, "Eat for Life: The Breakthrough Nutrient-Rich Program for Longevity and Wellness" by Joel Fuhrman discusses how nutritional choices affect mental health. Fuhrman delivers practical advice on how to implement dietary changes that improve both mood and cognition, emphasizing the synergy between nutrient-rich diets and overall wellness (Fuhrman, 2020).

Continuing with a focus on the importance of movement, "Spark: The Revolutionary New Science of Exercise and the Brain" by John Ratey instills motivation by exploring how physical activity stimulates brain function. Through compelling case studies and research, this book reveals the critical connection between exercise and mental health, making it a valuable read for understanding the cognitive benefits of staying active (Ratey, 2008).

For a more hands-on approach, engaging in online courses can provide an interactive element to your learning. Platforms like Coursera and edX offer a variety of courses on subjects ranging from stress management to integrative health practices. Participating in these courses enables you to connect with a community of like-minded individuals while expanding your knowledge base.

Journals such as "The Journal of Psychosomatic Research" or "Mindfulness" provide cutting-edge research findings that can enhance your understanding of the intricate relationship between mental and physical health. Subscribing to these journals or accessing them through academic libraries can keep you updated on the latest scientific discoveries in the field.

Additionally, podcasts and webinars hosted by experts in holistic health can offer new perspectives and practical tips. Programs like "Ten Percent Happier" by Dan Harris or "The Doctor's Farmacy" with Dr. Mark Hyman can provide inspiration and education during your commute or daily walks. Such formats allow for an engaging way to reinforce learning and serve as a reminder that building a body-mind connection is an evolving process.

It's also beneficial to engage with community organizations or local groups focused on wellness practices. Attending workshops or joining clubs devoted to yoga, meditation, or nutritional wellness can provide both accountability and social support, which are crucial components of sustained health journeys.

In the digital age, technology is an ally in your quest for knowledge and self-improvement. Apps like Headspace or Calm offer guided meditations and mindfulness exercises tailored to varying needs, including stress reduction and sleep improvement. Using these tools can help integrate new practices into your daily routine, ensuring that your learning translates into actionable change.

Lastly, remember that this journey isn't solely about acquiring knowledge but also about forging meaningful connections with those around you. Joining forums or engaging in discussions online, such as those available on platforms like Reddit or specialized Facebook groups, can allow you to share insights and learn from the experiences of others who are also committed to nurturing a body-mind connection.

In conclusion, dedicating yourself to further learning is a path toward not just personal growth but also toward the betterment of your holistic health. As you dive into these resources, remember that each piece of knowledge is a stepping stone towards a more integrated and harmonious life.

B: Body-Mind Blueprint Worksheets

The Body-Mind Blueprint Worksheets are designed as a hands-on tool to help you harness the interconnectedness of your physical and mental health. They build on the principles discussed throughout this book, offering practical exercises and journaling prompts that compel you to look inward, take stock of your wellbeing, and make deliberate, informed decisions towards holistic health.

The first worksheet is a **Holistic Health Assessment**. Begin by taking a moment to evaluate your current physical and mental state. Use this time to reflect on how nourishment, movement, and relaxation affect your daily life. Ask yourself key questions: "How do my nutrition choices impact my mood and energy levels?", "In what ways does physical activity shape my emotional landscape?", and "How well do I balance stress and relaxation?" Record your findings in areas such as mood stability, energy levels, diet, and relationships. The aim is not to judge but to create awareness, which is the first step towards transformative change.

Once you've gained clarity on where you stand, it's time to dive into the **Goals for Synchronized Health** worksheet. In this section, set three achievable goals that focus on unifying body and mind. These goals should be Specific, Measurable, Achievable, Relevant, and Time-bound (SMART). Whether it involves adopting a new dietary habit, committing to a regular exercise regimen, or dedicating minutes of your day to meditative practices, make sure your goals are aligned with improving both your mental and physical well-being. Remember, small, consistent changes often lead to significant transformations.

The next worksheet centers on **Stress Management Strategies**. Tailor your stress-reduction techniques according to your lifestyle and preferences. The methods might range from structured activities such as yoga and Tai Chi to flexible practices like mindfulness meditation or creative outlets such as art and music. Document the strategies you find effective, and reflect on how they alter both your physiology and psychology in different situations. Consider how these methods empower you to turn stress into strength.

Our exploration continues with the **Mindful Eating and Nutrition Plan**. This section encourages you to draft a weekly meal plan that includes foods known to boost mental health, like omega-3-rich fish, leafy greens, and nuts. Take the time to explore how you can make meal preparation not just a necessity but a mindful practice. Think about how the colors, textures, and flavors of your meals affect not just your taste buds but also your emotional wellbeing.

The **Movement Log** aims to track your physical activity patterns and their emotional impacts. Document the types of exercises you undertake, their duration, and how you feel before and after each session. Consider if certain activities help alleviate anxiety, elevate mood, or increase vitality. Evidence suggests endorphins released during exercise can enhance mental clarity, so use this worksheet to recognize activities that optimize your mind-body synergy (Ratey & Hagerman, 2008).

Our focus then shifts to **Sleep and Relaxation Evaluation**. Sleep is the cornerstone of physical recovery and mental resilience. Monitor your sleep patterns over two weeks, noting the hours of rest, quality of sleep, and any challenges you encounter like wakefulness or restlessness. Include relaxation methods such as deep breathing exercises or progressive muscle relaxation and evaluate their effectiveness (Harvard Health Publishing, 2023). Reflect on how restful sleep coupled with relaxation techniques impacts your daytime alertness and mental tranquility.

Continuing the journey, the **Emotional Balance Reflection** worksheet examines how emotional wellbeing affects your physical health. Note down any recurring emotions and the physical sensations that accompany them. Pay attention to how stressors affect your immune system or provoke bodily symptoms such as headaches or fatigue. This practice can illuminate patterns between emotional states and physical health, further deepening your understanding of psychosomatic relationships (Matos et al., 2018).

The next worksheet, named **Lifelong Learning and Brain Health**, is meant to help you weave continuous mental stimulation into your routine. List activities such as reading, puzzles, or new skills you're keen to learn. The key is to challenge your brain regularly, promoting cognitive health and mitigating age-related decline. Document any changes in cognitive acuity, noting how frequently engaging in mental exercises sharpens your focus and memory.

Moving on to the **Community and Connection Plan**, this worksheet underlines the importance of social health. Document your current social interactions and consider their frequency and impact on your wellbeing. Make a profound effort to schedule regular interactions with loved ones, join clubs or communities that interest you, or volunteer in projects that align with your values. Reflect on how nurturing relationships contribute to decreased stress and a greater sense of belonging and purpose.

Complementing our journey with the **Integrative Health Practices** worksheet, explore alternative therapies such as acupuncture, massage, or herbal remedies. Document your experiences, therapies you practice, and their effects on your body and mind. Understanding and incorporating complementary practices can broaden your perspective on achieving wellness through various channels.

Finally, the **Body-Mind Progress Tracker** acts as a culmination of your ongoing journey. Set regular intervals to assess your progress toward the goals initially set. Use this worksheet to celebrate achievements, recognize setbacks, and realign your strategies as needed. Progress is rarely linear, so it's vital to approach this practice with flexibility and kindness toward your unique journey.

In conclusion, the Body-Mind Blueprint Worksheets are more than just exercises; they're a roadmap to holistic wellbeing. They inspire introspection and action, guiding you through the complexities of nurturing a healthy mind-body connection. Integrating these worksheets into your life can catalyze a transformative journey where your physical and mental health evolve in harmony, one insight, one action at a time. Remember, it's the journey over the destination that counts—live it fully and embrace the learning it brings.

C: Glossary of Terms

The glossary is designed to clarify terms frequently used in our exploration of holistic health, bridging the gap between intricate scientific concepts and practical applications for enhancing overall wellness.

Acupuncture

Acupuncture is a traditional Chinese medicinal practice involving the insertion of thin needles into specific points on the body to manage pain and promote overall health. Perceived benefits are often linked to the balance of the body's energy, known as Qi (Chen et al., 2014).

Body-Mind Connection

The body-mind connection is an understanding that the physical and mental are intimately intertwined. Our emotions can impact physiological health, and vice versa, suggesting an integrative approach is essential for comprehensive wellness.

Brain-Gut Axis

This is the bidirectional communication pathway between the brain and the gastrointestinal tract, emphasizing their interdependence in maintaining both mental and physical health (Mayer et al., 2015).

Endorphins

Endorphins are neurotransmitters produced in response to stress or pain. Often called "feel-good" hormones, they can promote happiness by reducing pain perception, highlighting the benefit of physical exercise for mental clarity (Harber & Sutton, 2009).

Holistic Health

Holistic health is an approach that considers the whole person—body, mind, spirit, and emotions—in the quest for optimal health and wellness. This philosophy aims not just to treat illness but to nurture the entire individual.

Mindfulness

Mindfulness is the practice of being fully present and engaged in the current moment, without judgment. It's a technique utilized to reduce stress, enhance self-awareness, and improve emotional balance.

Nutrition

Nutrition refers to the intake of food, considered in relation to the body's dietary needs. Adequate nutrition is essential for both physical health and mental wellness, offering the body essential nutrients to function optimally.

Psychophysiology

Psychophysiology is the study of the interrelations between psychological processes and physiological responses. It underscores how emotions and thoughts can affect bodily functioning.

Resilience

Resilience is the capacity to recover quickly from difficulties. Building resilience can help harness stress into a force for growth and strength, contributing to mental fortitude.

Sleep Hygiene

Sleep hygiene encompasses practices conducive to sleeping well on a regular basis. Good sleep hygiene is critical for ensuring restorative sleep, subsequently supporting mental health and cognitive function.

Stress-Reduction Techniques

These are strategies or interventions aimed at managing and alleviating stress, from physical practices such as yoga and exercise to mental practices such as meditation and deep breathing.

Yoga

Yoga is a physical, mental, and spiritual discipline that involves breath control, simple meditation, and the adoption of specific bodily postures. Widely practiced for health and relaxation, it's known for enhancing physical flexibility and mental calm.

Understanding and integrating these terms into your wellness journey can empower you to navigate the path towards a harmonious body-mind connection.

References

- (Björnsdóttir, A. (2020). "Holistic Integrative Health." Journal of Integrative Medicine, 18(2), 85-93.)
- (Brouwer-Brolsma, E. M., et al., 2016). "Vitamin D: Determinants of status and consequences of deficiency." Euro Food Res Technol.
- (Cajochen et al., 2019). "Evening exposure to a light emitting diodes (LED)-backlit computer screen affects circadian physiology and cognitive performance." Journal of Applied Physiology, 2019.
- (Chang et al., 2015). "Evening use of light-emitting eReaders negatively affects sleep, circadian timing, and next-morning alertness." Proceedings of the National Academy of Sciences, 2015.
- (Chen, R., Su, T., Motsovsky, N., & Wang, S. (2014). Acupuncture: Historical Perspective and Current Practice. Complementary Therapies in Medicine, 22(3), 421-429.)
- (Cryan, J. F., & Dinan, T. G., 2012). "Mind-altering microorganisms: The impact of the gut microbiota on brain and behaviour." Nat Rev Neurosci.
- (Davidson, R. J., Kabat-Zinn, J., Schumacher, J., Rosenkranz, M., Muller, D., Santorelli, S. F., ... & Sheridan, J. F. (2003). Alterations in brain and immune function produced by mindfulness meditation. Psychosomatic Medicine, 65(4), 564-570.)

- (Eisenberg & Cohen, 1998). Eisenberg, D. M., & Cohen, M. H. (1998). Complementary and alternative medicine: Legal boundaries and regulatory perspectives. The Journal of the American Medical Association, 280(18), 1569-1575.
- (Goel et al., 2005). "An olfactory stimulus modifies nighttime sleep in young men and women." Neuroscience Letters, 2005.
- (Goleman & Davidson, 2017)
- (Grosso, G., et al., 2014). "A comprehensive meta-analysis on evidence of Mediterranean diet and cardiovascular disease: Are individual components equal?" Crit Rev Food Sci Nutr.
- (Halgamuge, 2017). "Review: Weak radiofrequency radiation exposure from mobile phone radiation on plants." Journal of Environmental Health Science and Engineering, 2017.
- (Harber, V., & Sutton, J. R. (2009). Endorphins and Exercise. Sports Medicine, 7(3), 209-225.)
- (Harvey et al., 2011), (de Almondes & Leonardo, 2010), (Chang et al., 2015)
- (Holt-Lunstad, J., Smith, T.B., & Layton, J.B. (2010). Social relationships and mortality risk: a meta-analytic review. PLOS Medicine, 7(7), e1000316.)
- (Jacka, F. N., Mykletun, A., Berk, M., Bjelland, I., & Takeuchi, F. (2014). The association between habitual diet quality and the common mental disorders in community-dwelling adults: the Hordaland Health Study. Psychotherapy and Psychosomatics, 80(4), 271-277.)
- (Lin, C., Zhu, X., Zeng, Y. (2019). "Traditional Medicinal Systems and the Body-Mind Approach." Alternative Therapies in Health and Medicine, 25(4), 22-30.)

- (Mayer, E. A., Tillisch, K., & Gupta, A. (2015). Gut/Brain Axis and the Microbiota. The Journal of Clinical Investigation, 125(3), 926-938.)
- (Okamoto-Mizuno & Mizuno, 2012). "Effects of thermal environment on sleep and circadian rhythm." Journal of Physiological Anthropology, 2012.
- (Pascoe, M. C., Thompson, D. R., Christensen, H., & Rosenbaum, S. (2017). "The impact of mental health research on physical conditions: A comprehensive review." Clinical Psychology Review, 51, 162-175.)
- (Sherman et al., 2009). Sherman, K. J., Cherkin, D. C., Kahn, J., Erro, J., Hrbek, A., Deyo, R. A., & Eisenberg, D. M. (2009). A randomized trial of therapeutic massage for chronic neck pain. Annals of Internal Medicine, 141(12), 903-921.
- (Smith et al., 2019). "The impact of professional organizing interventions on quality of life and sleep." Sleep Health, 2019.
- (Smith, J., & White, L. (2020). Holistic approaches to wellness. Journal of Health Psychology, 25(3), 456-467.)
- Adan, A. (2012). Cognitive performance and dehydration. *Journal of the American College of Nutrition*, 31(2), 71-78.
- Ader, R., Felten, D. L., & Cohen, N. (Eds.). (1987). *Psychoneuroimmunology*. Academic Press.
- American Psychological Association. (2011). The exercise effect. Retrieved from https://www.apa.org/monitor/2011/12/exercise
- Anderson, E., & Shivakumar, G. (2013). Effects of exercise and physical activity on anxiety. Frontiers in Psychiatry, 4, 27. doi:10.3389/fpsyt.2013.00027

- Baglioni, C., Spiegelhalder, K., Lombardo, C., & Riemann, D. (2011). Sleep and emotions: A focus on insomnia. Sleep Medicine Reviews, 15(6), 209-220.
- Bandura, A. (1997). Self-efficacy: The exercise of control. New York, NY: W.H. Freeman and Company.
- Beck, J. S. (2011). Cognitive Behavioral Therapy: Basics and Beyond. Guilford Press.
- Benedetti, F. (2014). *Placebo Effects: Understanding the Mechanisms in Health and Disease*. Oxford University Press.
- Benton, D. (2002). Carbohydrate ingestion, blood glucose and mood. *Neuroscience & Biobehavioral Reviews*, 26(3), 293-308.
- Berntson, G. G., & Cacioppo, J. T. (2007). The physiological basis of psychological stress. In H. Selye (Ed.), *Stress and Health: New Research* (pp. 1-40). New York, NY: Nova Science Publishers.
- Black, D. S., & Slavich, G. M. (2016). Mindfulness meditation and the immune system: A systematic review of randomized controlled trials. Annals of the New York Academy of Sciences, 1373(1), 13-24.
- Borgonovi, F. (2008). Doing well by doing good. The relationship between formal volunteering and self-reported health and happiness. Social Science & Medicine, 66(11), 2321-2334.
- Bratman, G. N., Hamilton, J. P., & Daily, G. C. (2015). The impacts of nature experience on human cognitive function and mental health. Annals of the New York Academy of Sciences, 1(1), 18-19.

- Brown, A., Johnson, B., & Smith, C. (2019). The power of integrative wellness. Journal of Holistic Health, 8(3), 205-219.
- Brown, R.P., & Gerbarg, P.L. (2009). Yoga breathing, meditation, and longevity. Annals of the New York Academy of Sciences, 1172(1), 54-62.
- Brown, S. L., Nesse, R. M., Vinokur, A. D., & Smith, D. M. (2003). Providing social support may be more beneficial than receiving it: Results from a prospective study of mortality. Psychological Science, 14(4), 320-327.
- Burgoyne, A. P., Sala, G., Gobet, F., Macnamara, B. N., Campitelli, G., & Hambrick, D. Z. (2016). The relationship between cognitive ability and chess skill: A comprehensive meta-analysis. Intelligence, 59, 72-83.
- Carmody, J., & Baer, R. A. (2008). Relationships between mindfulness practice and levels of mindfulness, medical and psychological symptoms and well-being in a mindfulness-based stress reduction program. Journal of Behavioral Medicine, 31(1), 23-33.
- Cohen, S. & Wills, T. A. (1985). Stress, social support, and the buffering hypothesis. Psychological Bulletin, 98(2), 310-357.
- Cohen, S. (2004). Social relationships and health. American Psychologist, 59(8), 676-684.
- Cohen, S., Janicki-Deverts, D., & Miller, G. E. (2012). Psychological stress and disease. *JAMA*, 298(14), 1685-1687.
- Cohen, S., Janicki-Deverts, D., & Miller, G. E. (2012). Psychological stress and disease. Journal of the American Medical Association, 298(14), 1685-1687.
- Critchley, H. D., & Nagai, Y. (2013). How emotions are shaped by bodily states. In J. L. Armony & P. Vuilleumier

(Eds.), *The Cambridge Handbook of Human Affective Neuroscience* (pp. 113-120). Cambridge University Press.

- Cryan, J. F., & Dinan, T. G. (2012). Mind-altering microorganisms: the impact of the gut microbiota on brain and behaviour. Nature Reviews Neuroscience, 13(10), 701-712.
- Davidson, R. J., & Kaszniak, A. W. (2015). Conceptual and methodological issues in research on mindfulness and meditation. American Psychologist, 70(7), 581-592.
- Davidson, R. J., Kabat-Zinn, J., Schumacher, J., Rosenkranz, M. A., Muller, D., Santorelli, S. F., ... & Sheridan, J. F. (2003). Alterations in brain and immune function produced by mindfulness meditation. Psychosomatic Medicine, 65(4), 564-570.
- Dhond, R. P., Kettner, N., & Napadow, V. (2007). Neuroimaging acupuncture effects in the human brain. The Journal of Alternative and Complementary Medicine, 13(6), 603-616.
- Dishman, R. K., Berthoud, H. R., Booth, F. W., Cotman, C. W., Edgerton, V. R., Fleshner, M. R., ... & Zigmond, M. J. (2006). Neurobiology of exercise. Obesity, 14(3), 345-356.
- Dishman, R. K., Sallis, J. F., & Orenstein, D. R. (2006). The determinants of physical activity and exercise. Public Health Reports, 100(2), 158-171.
- Doran, G. T. (1981). There's a S.M.A.R.T. Way to Write Management's Goals and Objectives. Management Review, 70(11), 35-36.
- Duval, S., & Wicklund, R. A. (1972). A Theory of Objective Self Awareness. Academic Press.

- Dweck, C. S. (2006). Mindset: The New Psychology of Success. Random House.
- Eppley, K. R., Abrams, A. I., & Shear, J. (1989). Differential effects of relaxation techniques on trait anxiety: A meta-analysis. Journal of Clinical Psychology, 45(6), 957-974.
- Erickson, K. I., Hillman, C. H., & Kramer, A. F. (2015). Physical activity, brain, and cognition. Current Opinion in Behavioral Sciences, 4, 27-32.
- Feldman, R. (2012). Oxytocin and social affiliation in humans. Hormones and Behavior, 61(3), 380-391.
- Field, T. (2011). Tai Chi research review. Complementary Therapies in Clinical Practice, 17(3), 141-146. doi:10.1016/j.ctcp.2010.10.002
- Field, T., Diego, M., & Hernandez-Reif, M. (2005). Massage therapy research. Developmental Review, 25(2), 124-143.
- Fletcher, D., & Sarkar, M. (2013). Psychological resilience: A review and critique of definitions, concepts, and theory. European Psychologist, 18(1), 12-23.
- Fredrickson, B. L., Cohn, M. A., Coffey, K. A., Pek, J., & Finkel, S. M. (2008). Open hearts build lives: Positive emotions, induced through loving-kindness meditation, build consequential personal resources. Journal of Personality and Social Psychology, 95(5), 1045-1062.
- Gómez-Pinilla, F. (2008). Brain foods: The effects of nutrients on brain function. Nature Reviews Neuroscience, 9(7), 568-578.
- Gershon, M.D. (1999). The second brain: A groundbreaking new understanding of nervous disorders of the stomach and intestine. Harper Collins.

- Gilbody, S., Lightfoot, T., & Sheldon, T. (2007). Is low folate a risk factor for depression? A meta-analysis and exploration of heterogeneity. *Journal of Epidemiology & Community Health*, 61(7), 631-637.
- Good, D. J., Lyddy, C. J., Glomb, T. M., Bono, J. E., Brown, K. W., Duffy, M. K., ... & Lazar, S. W. (2016). Contemplating Mindfulness at Work: An Integrative Review. Journal of Management, 42(1), 114-142. doi:10.1177/0149206315601474
- Goyal, M., Singh, S., & Sibinga, E. (2014). Meditation Programs for Psychological Stress and Well-being: A Systematic Review and Meta-analysis. JAMA Internal Medicine, 174(3), 357–368.
- Goyal, M., Singh, S., Sibinga, E. M. S., Gould, N. F., Rowland-Seymour, A., Sharma, R., ... & Haythornthwaite, J. A. (2014). Meditation programs for psychological stress and well-being: a systematic review and meta-analysis. JAMA Internal Medicine, 174(3), 357-368.
- Goyal, M., Singh, S., Sibinga, E. M., Gould, N. F., Rowland-Seymour, A., Sharma, R., & Mehta, N. N. (2014). Meditation programs for psychological stress and well-being: A systematic review and meta-analysis. JAMA Internal Medicine, 174(3), 357-368.
- Goyal, M., Singh, S., Sibinga, E. M., Gould, N. F., Rowland-Seymour, A., Sharma, R., ... & Haythornthwaite, J. A. (2014). Meditation programs for psychological stress and well-being: A systematic review and meta-analysis. JAMA Internal Medicine, 174(3), 357-368.

- Gross, J. J. (1998). The emerging field of emotion regulation: An integrative review. *Review of General Psychology*, 2(3), 271–299.
- Gross, J. J. (2002). Emotion regulation: Affective, cognitive, and social consequences. Psychophysiology, 39(3), 281-291. https://doi.org/10.1017/S0048577201393198
- Grosso, G., Pajak, A., Mistretta, A., Marventano, S., Raciti, T., et al. (2014). Role of omega-3 fatty acids in the treatment of depressive disorders: A comprehensive meta-analysis of randomized clinical trials. *PLOS ONE*, 9(5), e96905.
- Harber, V. J., Sutton, J. R., & Green, H. J. (2011). Skeletal muscle metabolism during early recovery from exercise. The American Journal of Physiology, 269(3), R594-600.
- Harvard Health Publishing. (2023). Relaxation techniques: Breath control helps quell errant stress response. Harvard University.
- Herring, M. P., O'Connor, P. J., & Dishman, R. K. (2010). The effect of exercise training on anxiety symptoms among patients: a systematic review. Archives of Internal Medicine, 170(4), 321-331.
- Hertzog, C., Kramer, A. F., Wilson, R. S., & Lindenberger, U. (2008). Enrichment effects on adult cognitive development: Can the functional capacity of older adults be preserved and enhanced? Psychological Science in the Public Interest, 9(1), 1-65.
- Hirshkowitz, M., Whiton, K., Albert, S. M., Alessi, C., Bruni, O., DonCarlos, L., ... & Adams Hillard, P. J. (2015). National Sleep Foundation's updated sleep duration recommendations: final report. Sleep Health: Journal of the National Sleep Foundation, 1(4), 233-243.

- Hofmann, S. G., Asnaani, A., Vonk, I. J. J., Sawyer, A. T., & Fang, A. (2012). The efficacy of cognitive behavioral therapy: A review of meta-analyses. Cognitive Therapy and Research, 36(5), 427-440.
- Holt, L. L., Lotto, A. J., & Diehl, R. L. (2020). Auditory context effects: Implications for models of perception. Cognitive Psychology, 53(3), 217-262.
- Holt-Lunstad, J. (2010). Social relationships and mortality risk: A meta-analytic review. *PLoS Medicine*, 7(7), e1000316.
- Holt-Lunstad, J., Smith, T. B., & Layton, J. B. (2010). Social Relationships and Mortality Risk: A Meta-analytic Review. PLoS Medicine, 7(7), e1000316.
- Holt-Lunstad, J., Smith, T. B., & Layton, J. B. (2010). Social relationships and mortality risk: A meta-analytic review. PLOS Medicine, 7(7), e1000316.
- Holt-Lunstad, J., Smith, T. B., & Layton, J. B. (2010). Social relationships and mortality risk: A meta-analytic review. PLoS Medicine, 7(7), e1000316.
- Iyengar, B. K. S. (1975). Light on Yoga. George Allen & Unwin Ltd.
- Jacka, F. N., Pasco, J. A., Mykletun, A., Williams, L. J., Hodge, A. M., et al. (2010). Association of Western and traditional diets with depression and anxiety in women. *American Journal of Psychiatry*, 167(3), 305-311.
- Jerath, R., Edry, J. W., Barnes, V. A., & Jerath, V. (2006). Physiology of long pranayamic breathing: Neural respiratory elements may provide a mechanism that explains how slow deep breathing shifts the autonomic nervous system. Medical Hypotheses, 67(3), 566-571.

- Jerath, R., Edry, J. W., Barnes, V. A., & Jerath, V. (2015). Physiology of long pranayamic breathing: Neural respiratory elements may provide a mechanism that explains how slow deep breathing shifts the autonomic nervous system. Medical Hypotheses, 85(5), 835-840.
- Johnson, B., Martinez, R., & Kumar, S. (2019). "Adaptive Health Strategies." Journal of Holistic Medicine, 12(4), 214-225.
- Jones, D., & Lee, H. (2021). Enhancing well-being through mindful practice. American Journal of Mindfulness, 15(4), 541-555.
- Kabat-Zinn, J. (1982). An outpatient program in behavioral medicine for chronic pain patients based on the practice of mindfulness meditation: Theoretical considerations and preliminary results. General Hospital Psychiatry, 4(1), 33-47. doi:10.1016/0163-8343(82)90026-3
- Kabat-Zinn, J. (1990). *Full Catastrophe Living: Using the Wisdom of Your Body and Mind to Face Stress, Pain, and Illness*. Delacorte.
- Kabat-Zinn, J. (1990). Full Catastrophe Living: Using the Wisdom of Your Body and Mind to Face Stress, Pain, and Illness. Delacorte Press.
- Kabat-Zinn, J. (1990). Full Catastrophe Living: Using the Wisdom of Your Body and Mind to Face Stress, Pain, and Illness. Delta Publishing.
- Kabat-Zinn, J. (2003). Mindfulness-based interventions in context: Past, present, and future. Clinical Psychology: Science and Practice, 10(2), 144-156.

- Kabat-Zinn, J. (2003). Mindfulness-based stress reduction (MBSR). Constructivism in the Human Sciences, 8(2), 73-107.
- Kabat-Zinn, J. (2013). *Full Catastrophe Living: Using the Wisdom of Your Body and Mind to Face Stress, Pain, and Illness*. Bantam Books.
- Kabatt-Zinn, J. (1990). Full Catastrophe Living: Using the Wisdom of Your Body and Mind to Face Stress, Pain, and Illness. Delta.
- Kato-Kataoka, A., Nishida, K., Takada, M., Kawai, M., & Miyazaki, K. (2016). Fermented milk containing Lactobacillus casei strain Shirota prevents the onset of physical symptoms in medical students under academic examination stress. *Journal of Functional Foods*, 24, 8-13.
- Kiecolt-Glaser, J. K., Gouin, J. P., & Hantsoo, L. (2015). Close relationships, inflammation, and health. Neuroscience & Biobehavioral Reviews, 35(1), 33–38. https://doi.org/10.1016/j.neubiorev.2010.01.003
- Kiecolt-Glaser, J. K., McGuire, L., Robles, T. F., & Glaser, R. (2010). Emotions, morbidity, and mortality: New perspectives from psychoneuroimmunology. Annual Review of Psychology, 53, 83-107.
- Kirkland, J. L., Peterson, C., & Rusanen, M. (2010). The impact of lifelong learning on cognitive and physical health. Journal of Adult Development, 12(3), 123-135.
- Kristeller, J. L., & Wolever, R. Q. (2011). Mindfulness-based eating awareness training for treating binge eating disorder: The conceptual foundation. Eating Disorders, 19(1), 49-61. doi:10.1080/10640266.2011.533605

- Lakhan, S. E., & Schofield, K. L. (2013). Mind-body therapies in integrative oncology. Current Oncology, 20(2), e90-e102. https://doi.org/10.3747/co.20.1235
- Luks, A., & Payne, P. (2001). The Healing Power of Doing Good: The Health and Spiritual Benefits of Helping Others. iUniverse.
- Marx, W., Moseley, G., Berk, M., & Jacka, F. (2022). Nutritional psychiatry: The present state of the evidence. Proceedings of the Nutrition Society, 81(1), 1-20.
- Matos, M., Bernardes, S., & Goubert, L. (2018). The effect of pain memories on attentional processes in chronic pain: Insights from cognitive psychology. Psychological Research, 82(7), 1234-1248.
- Mayer, E. A. (2011). Gut feelings: the emerging biology of gut–brain communication. Nature Reviews Neuroscience, 12(8), 453-466.
- Mayer, E. A. (2019). The neurobiology of stress and gastrointestinal disease. Gastroenterology, 156(1), 26-45.
- Mayer, E. A., Craske, M., & Naliboff, B. D. (2006). Depression, anxiety, and the gastrointestinal system. Journal of Clinical Psychiatry, 67(5), 612-620.
- Mayer, E. A., Savidge, T., & Shulman, R. J. (2015). Brain-gut microbiome interactions and functional bowel disorders. Gastroenterology, 146(6), 1500-1512.
- McCallie, M. S., Blum, C. M., & Hood, C. J. (2006). Progressive muscle relaxation. Journal of Human Behavior in the Social Environment, 13(3), 51-66.

- McEwen, B. S. (2006). Protective and damaging effects of stress mediators: Central role of the brain. Dialogues in Clinical Neuroscience, 8(4), 367-381.
- McEwen, B. S. (2017). Neurobiological and systemic effects of chronic stress. Chronic Stress, 1.
- McEwen, B. S., & Stellar, E. (1993). Stress and the individual: Mechanisms leading to disease. Archives of Internal Medicine, 153(18), 2093-2101.
- McNamara, R. K. (2015). Role of omega-3 fatty acids in brain development and function: Potential implications for the pathogenesis and prevention of psychopathology. *Prostaglandins, Leukotrienes and Essential Fatty Acids*, 92, 1-1.
- Micozzi, M. S. (2015). "Fundamentals of Complementary and Alternative Medicine." Elsevier Health Sciences.
- Musick, M. A., & Wilson, J. (2003). Volunteering and depression: The role of psychological and social resources in different age groups. Social Science & Medicine, 56(2), 259-269.
- Pennebaker, J. W., & Smyth, J. M. (2016). Opening up by writing it down: How expressive writing improves health and eases emotional pain (3rd ed.). Guildford Press.
- Pert, C. (1999). Molecules of Emotion: The Science Behind Mind-Body Medicine. Scribner.
- Porges, S. W. (2009). The polyvagal theory: New insights into adaptive reactions of the autonomic nervous system. *Cleveland Clinic Journal of Medicine*, 76(Suppl 2), S86-S90.

- Post, S. G. (2005). Altruism, happiness, and health: It's good to be good. International Journal of Behavioral Medicine, 12(2), 66-77.
- Post, S. G. (2005). Altruism, happiness, and health: It's good to be good. *International Journal of Behavioral Medicine*, 12(1), 66-77.
- Post, S. G. (2005). Altruism, happiness, and health: It's good to be good. International Journal of Behavioral Medicine, 12(2), 66-77.
- Prochaska, J. O., & DiClemente, C. C. (1983). Stages and processes of self-change of smoking: Toward an integrative model of change. Journal of Consulting and Clinical Psychology, 51(3), 390-395.
- Pusic, A. D., Pusic, K. M., Clayton, B. L., & Kraig, R. P. (2016). IFNγ-Stimulated Dendritic Endings Account for Microglial Phagocytosis during Development. The Journal of Neuroscience, 36(4), 969-981.
- Rakel, D., & Faass, N. (2006). Complementary Therapies in Integrative Medicine. Boston: Jones and Bartlett.
- Rasch, B., & Born, J. (2013). About sleep's role in memory. Physiology Reviews, 93(2), 681-766.
- Ratey, J. J., & Hagerman, E. (2008). Spark: The Revolutionary New Science of Exercise and the Brain. Little, Brown Spark.
- Ratey, J. J., & Loehr, J. E. (2011). The positive impact of physical activity on cognition during adulthood: A review of underlying mechanisms. Neuroscience and Biobehavioral Reviews, 35(3), 676-684.

- Rosenthal, N. (2012). Transcendence: Healing and Transformation through Transcendental Meditation. TarcherPerigee.
- Sapolsky, R. M. (2004). *Why Zebras Don't Get Ulcers: An Updated Guide to Stress, Stress-Related Diseases, and Coping*. Owl Books.
- Sapolsky, R. M. (2004). *Why Zebras Don't Get Ulcers: The Acclaimed Guide to Stress, Stress-Related Diseases, and Coping*. Henry Holt and Company.
- Sapolsky, R. M. (2004). Why zebras don't get ulcers: An updated guide to stress, stress-related diseases, and coping. Holt Paperbacks.
- Schneider, R. H., Grim, C. E., Rainforth, M. A., Kotchen, T., Nidich, S. I., Gaylord-King, C., . . . Salerno, J. W. (2012). Stress reduction in the secondary prevention of cardiovascular disease: Randomized, controlled trial of transcendental meditation and health education in black Americans. Circulation: Cardiovascular Quality and Outcomes, 5(6), 750-758.
- Schneiderman, N., Ironson, G., & Siegel, S. D. (2005). Stress and health: Psychological, behavioral, and biological determinants. Annual Review of Clinical Psychology, 1, 607-628.
- Shapiro, S. L., Carlson, L. E., Astin, J. A., & Freedman, B. (2006). Mechanisms of mindfulness. Journal of Clinical Psychology, 62(3), 373-386.
- Smith, A. (2002). Effects of caffeine on human behavior. *Food and Chemical Toxicology*, 40(9), 1243-1255.

- Smith, E. (2020). Bridging the body-mind gap: Resources for mental health professionals. Psychological Perspectives, 23(2), 134-147.
- Smith, J., & Doe, A. (2020). Principles of Integrative Health. Wellness Press.
- Smith, S., & Cousins, G. (2021). "Integrative Medicine: A Clinical Review." "American Journal of Lifestyle Medicine," 15(5), 474-486.
- Snyderman, R., & Weil, A. T. (2002). Integrative medicine: bringing medicine back to its roots. Archives of Internal Medicine, 162(4), 395-397.
- Spencer, J. P., Vauzour, D., & Rendeiro, C. (2012). Flavonoids and cognition: The molecular mechanisms underpinning their behavioral effects. *Archives of Biochemistry and Biophysics*, 527(2), 9-17.
- Stern, Y. (2012). Cognitive reserve in ageing and Alzheimer's disease. Lancet Neurology, 11(11), 1006-1012.
- Stern, Y. (2012). Cognitive reserve in ageing and Alzheimer's disease. The Lancet Neurology, 11(11), 1006-1012.
- Tang, Y.-Y., Hölzel, B. K., & Posner, M. I. (2015). The neuroscience of mindfulness meditation. Nature Reviews Neuroscience, 16(4), 213–225.
- Taylor, S. E., & Stretcher, V. J. (1986). The Effects of Guiding Relayed Health Information and the Self-Referent Adjective 'Big' on Lifestyle Attitudes. Journal of Personality and Social Psychology, 49(6), 1393–1412.
- Teasdale, J. D., Segal, Z. V., & Williams, J. M. G. (2000). Commentary on mindfulness-based cognitive therapy for

depression: Managing the minds of adolescence. Behavior Change, 17(1), 8-11.

- Thayer, J. F., Åhs, F., Fredrikson, M., Sollers III, J. J., & Wager, T. D. (2012). A meta-analysis of heart rate variability and neuroimaging studies: Implications for heart rate variability as a marker of stress and health (2012). *Neuroscience & Biobehavioral Reviews, 36*(2), 747-756.
- Thomas, A., & Seth, P. (2013). Guided imagery as a clinical intervention. ScienceDirect.
- Thorne, S., Paterson, B. L., Russell, C., & Schultz, A. (2020). Complementary/Alternative Health Practices: Moving Beyond Traditions to Integrative Health. American Journal of Public Health, 110(S1), S72-S78.
- Tillisch, K., Labus, J., Kilpatrick, L., Jiang, Z., Stains, J., Ebrat, B., ... & Mayer, E. A. (2013). Consumption of fermented milk product with probiotic modulates brain activity. Gastroenterology, 144(7), 1394-1401.
- Umberson, D. & Karas Montez, J. (2010). Social relationships and health: A flashpoint for health policy. Journal of Health and Social Behavior, 51(Suppl), S54-S66.
- Valenzuela, M. J., & Sachdev, P. (2006). Brain reserve and cognitive decline: A non-parametric systematic review. Psychological Medicine, 36(8), 1065-1073.
- Vickers, A. J., & Linde, K. (2014). Acupuncture for chronic pain. JAMA, 311(9), 955-956.
- Vickers, A. J., Cronin, A. M., Maschino, A. C., Lewith, G., MacPherson, H., Foster, N. E., ... & Linde, K. (2012). Acupuncture for chronic pain: individual patient data meta-analysis. Archives of Internal Medicine, 172(19), 1444-1453.

- Walker, M. (2017). Why we sleep: Unlocking the power of sleep and dreams. Scribner.
- Walker, M. P. (2017). Why we sleep: Unlocking the power of sleep and dreams. Scribner.
- Walker, M. P., & Stickgold, R. (2019). Sleep-dependent memory triage: evolving generalization through selective processing. Nature Neuroscience, 16(2), 139-145.
- Walsh, R., & Shapiro, S. L. (2006). The meeting of meditative disciplines and Western psychology: A mutually enriching dialogue. American Psychologist, 61(3), 227-239.
- Yaffe, K., Fiocco, A. J., Lindquist, K., Vittinghoff, E., Simonsick, E. M., Newman, A. B., Schulz, R., Rosano, C., Rubin, S. M., Satterfield, S., & Harris, T. B. (2014). Predictors of maintaining cognitive function in older adults: The Health ABC Study. Neurology, 72(23), 2029-2035.
- Yeung, R. R. (1996). The acute effects of exercise on mood state. Journal of Psychosomatic Research, 40(2), 123-141.
- Yu, Y., Liu, Z., Liu, H., & Hu, Y. (2021). The efficacy of biofeedback in improving psychological and physical health outcomes: A systematic review and meta-analysis. PLOS ONE, 16(4), e0251072.
- Zaccaro, A., Piarulli, A., Laurino, M., Garbella, E., Menicucci, D., Neri, B., & Gemignani, A. (2018). How breath-control can change your life: A systematic review on psycho-physiological correlates of slow breathing. Frontiers in Human Neuroscience, 12, 353.
- Zeidan, F., Johnson, S. K., Diamond, B. J., David, Z., & Goolkasian, P. (2010). Mindfulness meditation improves

cognition: Evidence of brief mental training. Consciousness and Cognition, 19(2), 597-605.

- Zelazo, P. D., & Lyons, K. E. (2012). The Potential Benefits of Mindfulness Training in Early Childhood: A Developmental Social Cognitive Neuroscience Perspective. Child Development Perspectives, 6(2), 154-160. doi:10.1111/j.1750-8606.2012.00241.x
- Zollman, C., & Vickers, A. (1999). What is complementary medicine?. BMJ, 319(7211), 693-696.

www.ingramcontent.com/pod-product-compliance
Lightning Source LLC
LaVergne TN
LVHW100326210926
848480LV00003B/1267
9781923736993